BOOKS BY GUILLAUME WOLF "PROF. G"

- *You Are a Dream*
- *You Are a Message*
- *You Are a Circle*

For information about the author, creative workshops, and additional content, please visit **www.ProfG.co**

YOU ARE A DREAM

AN INTRODUCTION TO THE CREATIVE DREAMING METHOD

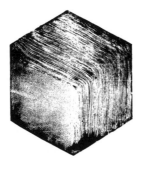

GUILLAUME WOLF "PROF. G"

FIRST EDITION

For Margaux,

with all my love

The greatest discovery of my generation is that a human being can alter his life by altering his attitudes of mind.

— **William James**

You never change things by fighting the existing reality.
To change something, build a new model that makes the existing model obsolete.

— **R. Buckminster Fuller**

Whatever you do, or dream you can, begin it. Boldness has genius and power and magic in it.

— **Johann Wolfgang von Goethe**

TABLE OF CONTENTS

A LETTER FOR YOU

Hello, my creative friend,

Let me ask you a question:

Have you ever experienced a moment in your life when you had a dream and took the steps to make it happen, and in doing so, succeeded in accomplishing something that everyone around you viewed as being "impossible"?

Of course, you have.

These moments (big or small) have happened to all of us, and they make the human experience vibrant and beautiful. In fact, this capacity for creating change—or more accurately, "transforming reality"—is a gift we all possess. And it always starts with an idea, a desire that grows within yourself. A dream that wants to be expressed in the world.

Yet, unfortunately, these precious moments are also very rare. They are hard to duplicate.

The art of dreaming up an idea and actualizing it into reality is completely unique because it challenges you to use reality as the ground for experimentation. When you create something and test it in the real world, *you* will be tested as well.

This book is an introduction to the **Creative Dreaming Method**, a unique approach to creating change by design. The goal of the Creative Dreaming Method is to answer a very important question:

How can I make my dreams come true and transform my current reality?

To answer this question meaningfully, the Creative Dreaming Method offers a way to study the relationship between creativity, self, and reality. Understanding how this relationship works is the key to making your dreams come true.

WHEN YOU CREATE, YOU MUTATE
Here, I'd like to share with you a secret about creativity:

Creativity is a transformative force that you can use to create change in the world. But it works only *if* you are willing to create change within yourself as well.

Creative Dreaming is always happening inside and outside, simultaneously.

Let's go back again to my first question . . . I've asked you to think about your life and recall a moment when you've accomplished *"something that everyone around you viewed as being 'impossible.'"* It could have been learning a difficult skill, picking up a new habit, or creating a change in your life.

You took the steps, and despite the odds, you succeeded.

And let me ask you this: Now that this accomplishment is behind you, in what way are you a different person today?

Think about it.

As you achieved your outside goal, an inner transformation took place as well. What in the past had seemed daring, or even "impossible" for the person you were back then is now a fact for the person you are today.

Although, on a superficial level, this seems to be just a "side effect" of outer change, it's not. Creative Dreaming is always about creating a new "you."

To put it simply: **When *you* create, *you* mutate.**

THIS IS YOUR PATH
We are all looking to get something from the experience of life.

And so, today, what do you want from your life?

While this is a straightforward question, it's a bit tricky to find a proper answer for it, isn't it?

Deep down, you just know that "something" is there for you. You know that, within your own life, there's a gem to be found. And finding it is perhaps why you have chosen the creative life to begin with.

As a creative, you are creating. As a creative, you are expressing your capacity to bring something new into the world. This means that with each creative gesture, you are revealing the unseen.

So here, for the sake of our conversation, I'm going to call this elusive gem happiness.

But again, what is happiness? There's not just one definition for it. Your gem is uniquely yours.

For some, happiness equals using self-expression to make

a difference; for others, it's living amazing experiences and memorable adventures.

For some, happiness equals nurturing quality relationships; for others, it's being the best you can be.

For some, happiness equals building a legacy that will have a positive impact on the future; for others, it's about contributing and about challenging the present.

And finally, for some, it's all of the above.

You see, my creative friend, there are billions of ways to walk on the road of happiness. One is never better than another. What's really important is to walk on your path—the path that's rewarding for *you*.

Your life is the perfect ground of experimentation for Creative Dreaming. A path on which to imagine and realize your vision—and in doing so, it's also an opportunity to grow and evolve.

MY MESSAGE
I don't know what's going on in your life today . . . or why you picked up this book. Maybe you're doing great and want to keep growing by exploring new ideas, or maybe you'd like to do better in one category, or two.

Here, I'd like to tell you that, regardless of where you are today, you have the capacity to find the gem in your own life and to build the compelling future that you want.

This is my message:
You can dream something beautiful and make it real.

A MAP FOR TRANSFORMATION AND GROWTH

The act of creating is twofold: It takes place outside, when you take the steps to actualize your idea into the real world; and it also takes place inside, when you grow into the kind of person who can make this idea happen—and sustain it.

Inside and outside—Creative Dreaming is about authentic transformation and growth.

This book is a primer to the **Creative Dreaming Method**, and it includes every step of the creative process. It will show you a new map to help you make your ideas come true—to become a Creative Dreamer.

WARNING

A friendly warning: What you're going to discover here is going to challenge you. It's going to challenge you on every level.

The ideas described in *You Are a Dream* will question many assumptions, beliefs, and cultural biases about creativity.

Together, we're about to go on an incredible journey. We're going to learn thought-provoking ideas inspired by science, ancient traditions, cybernetics, and cutting-edge design processes.

This book is a manual for change; it's also a manual for inner transformation.

Some of these ideas will ask you to look at reality (and yourself) from a completely different perspective. So please, brace yourself.

Our conversation will start with you and Life (with a big "L"). The reason is simple: In order to start dreaming, creating, and expressing yourself fully and successfully in the world, we first need to have a working model of how the world works. Therefore, to begin our journey, we need to start building a map.

FROM MACRO TO MICRO
The Creative Dreaming Method is modeled as a guiding map. And this map comes with a big disclaimer—to quote **Alfred Korzybski**, *"the map is not the territory."*

Therefore, the work presented here simply offers a model—a point of view. It doesn't claim to hold any absolute "truth." And if you connect with these ideas, you'll get to decide if you want to implement them and see if they work for you. This is important because the Method is not here to tell you how to live your life—that's obviously your job. To be truly yours, your dream must be created around your values, not someone else's.

However, throughout the book I will ask you to make sure that your dream is what I call "happy/healthy." This means simply that pursuing your dream (even if it's hard) creates joy and goodwill in your life and in the lives of people around you.

In order to learn about the Creative Dreaming Method, we're first going to look at Life from a macro perspective (large scale), and then we will zoom into the micro (your life).

In **Part 1, The Big Picture**, we'll start with the **10.10 Principles**. These ideas are going to be the backbone for the rest of our conversation. These principles will help us focus our thinking by setting up a solid frame of reference as we move forward. Next, I'll ask you to put your philosopher's hat on to think about Life and your place in it. We're going to take the time to "think about your thinking" and create the space to ask a very important—and timeless—philosophical question: *"Who are you?"* This first part might be the most challenging, as I will ask you to look at your life (and yourself) from a different perspective, one where creativity becomes the driving force and the source of your experiences.

In **Part 2**, **Obstacles**, we're going to take a look at the many walls you'll find in front of you as you walk along the creative path. This section will give you a clear view and understanding of the challenges connected with the creative process, and how to overcome them.

And in **Part 3**, **Creative Dreaming**, we'll go ahead and discuss creative strategies you can implement in your own life to dream big dreams and actualize them into the world.

At the end of the book you'll also discover the transcript of a late-night **Conversation** about Creative Dreaming.

IS THE CREATIVE DREAMING METHOD FOR YOU?
So now, you might wonder: *"Is the Creative Dreaming Method for me?"*

I'm going to be very direct: I don't know.

You see, Creative Dreaming is *not* for everybody. What I can tell you is that Creative Dreaming is for the creative soul who is willing to confront the status quo from within and without. Creative Dreaming is for the bold.

And as a teacher, I'm an advocate for authentic transformation and growth, not quick fixes.

In preparing this project, I've made the choice to talk to you, the reader, as I would talk to a friend—as honestly as possible. I'm diving deep into a new territory that's very challenging, and I'm asking tough questions. Nothing here is sugarcoated.

What I can tell you is that successful Creative Dreaming starts with a desire, a curiosity, or a thirst for something that's not there. Next, it's followed by an inner resolve—a powerful decision. A commitment to create, no matter what.

And if this is you, simply bring this energy and explore with an open mind.

If you do, I'd like to welcome you to the Creative Dreaming Method. I'm really looking forward to sharing these ideas with you. And please, always remember that it doesn't matter where (or when) you start—creativity is always all-inclusive.

You're never too old or too young. You're never too big or too small. Just come as you are, today.

WHY I WROTE THIS BOOK

This book, *You Are a Dream* (2017), is the third volume of a body of work I started with *You Are a Circle* (2012), followed by *You Are a Message* (2015). Initially, the project began with the simple concept of sharing some thoughts about life and creativity with my daughter, Margaux (she's five now), as a form of "love legacy." Something she'll be able to take a look at years from now—like a little time capsule. And as the books started receiving positive support from the creative community, I slowly began realizing that these ideas were needed on a larger scale, and the project evolved organically.

But that's not all . . .

The ideas you'll find here are the by-product of a life practice dedicated to creativity. A life filled with ups and downs, with incredible obstacles and breakthroughs, and, more importantly, with ongoing learning experiences, growth, successes, and happiness.

Everything I have in my life today—my beautiful family, my creative career, my teaching practice, and my health—I owe to the Creative Dreaming Method. This practice—imagining the new in order to make it real—and the growth discipline that comes with it, has been a true blessing.

But guess what? . . . I should never have been able to live this rich, creative life to begin with.

I grew up in Paris, France. At an early age, I was labeled "educationally challenged," and promptly kicked out of the French public school system and oriented toward menial work.

Later, as I was sharing positive plans to create change in my own life—imagining what creative living would look like—I was constantly told that my ideas and aspirations were impossible, that I was "just a dreamer."

At age eighteen, with little education, living in a time when unemployment was on the rise, my life was pretty bleak. Many of my friends were involved in drugs. There was little hope or excitement. It was a very dark time. Yet I would try to imagine possibilities. I would say things that sounded silly. Things like: *"I wonder what it would be like to live close to nature? What if I moved away from Paris and the grayness, and tried something different—maybe lived in California?"* And of course, over and over, I kept hearing the same comments: *"Stop dreaming—that can't be done. What you're talking about doesn't exist."*

I was surrounded by walls.

This constant denial of the possibility of growth and change felt like a prison. I was living in a state of frustration, craving a new life. And this is what prompted me to search for knowledge.

As a young adult, I had the intuition that creativity was a force for change that went beyond the limits of the arts. I knew instinctively that creative skills were connected to one's own life, and on a larger scale, society and the world. This belief made me want to know more, and cracking the code of creativity became my life's mission.

Because, you see, my creative friend, even after my first breakthrough and the following years of creative success working as a visual artist, I still faced the same walls: people, or situations, that all said, *"This is impossible."* So I refined my research. I kept at it.

I have a love for books, and I decided early on to educate myself through reading—devouring everything I could get my hands on. I was also lucky to meet incredible creatives who took me under their wings and became my mentors.

And after decades upon decades of inquiry, I did find something. There was a secret, indeed.

And this secret was more profound than what I originally imagined. Encountering it was a deep, humbling experience. It forced me to reevaluate everything, from how I looked at life to how I looked at myself.

This encounter changed me, and changed everything around me. I was transformed inside and out.

At first, I used my discoveries to create the life I wanted—and it felt like magic. Starting from a place where I was trapped in a cycle of ups and downs, I moved into a living flow where love, work, health, and relationships came together as one. Then I began sharing these ideas with others, and I saw the same results happening in their lives, too.

Over the years, I've organized these discoveries into a workable system; this is how I created the Creative Dreaming Method.

And today, I'm what you could call a "change agent."

After more than two decades of living a joyful and rewarding creative career over two continents, I'm now a teacher, an associate professor, working at one of the best design colleges in the world.

In my daily life, I have the incredible privilege of training the next generation of creatives. I also work with brands and non-profit organizations to help them solve creative problems and dream big dreams.

Finally, through my books, I have the pleasure of connecting with readers like you and, through these conversations, creating a space in which we can talk about creativity and life.

I'm sharing my story with you because I'm living proof that, no matter where you start, creativity can help you make the impossible possible.

Today, as I'm writing these words, I'm sitting at my desk, inside my mountain home in beautiful Lake Arrowhead, California. Outside, I can see majestic pine trees and giant sequoias. I hear the melody of wild birds. Inside, I feel the radiating heat from the wood-burning stove. Upstairs, my daughter is playing. Downstairs, my wife (my love) is working in her studio. I have a hard time believing all this is real. But it is.

Every day, I wake up grateful.

On a personal level, the practice of Creative Dreaming has not only helped me create the life I imagined; it has also made me grow into a better person (and it still does, every single day). It has provided my life with meaning—giving me an invaluable life ethic filled with hope, certainty, and joy. More important, Creative Dreaming has helped me make a difference in the world—contributing to the lives of others.

The Creative Dreaming Method has revealed a living world in which everything is interconnected. A world where, together, we can all succeed. A world where fear of each other has been replaced by love of each other.

A utopia?

No, a new reality. An operating, creative way of life that you can be a part of, today.

In this world of possibilities, you'll find that your life

can be rekindled by the present moment—right here, *right now*. You'll find that by taking a new perspective, you can become a force for change.

You'll find that you can dream with *certainty*.

So here's why I really wrote this book, my creative friend:
I found something beautiful, and I'd like to share it with you.

WE NEED TO EVOLVE
As you know, my creative friend, we live in complicated times.

We are all participating in a so-called "modern" world that's anything but modern. The dream of collective progress has let us down. It has been substituted by a lifeless, automated world that turns out to be without values or meaning: a strange spiritual vacuum. This is a place where individual lives are regimented by mathematical models and algorithms, where every relationship is based on either a transaction or a power play. And of course, in this automated world, the individual is treated as an automaton.

Once, progress meant exploring and growing *together* as a human race. It meant creating a compelling future *for all of us*. Today, progress means quantifying every aspect of human life through cold data.

We're left with no moral support, wisdom, love, or vision. By refusing to evolve, traditional institutions have shied away from their responsibility to provide us with significant answers. Meanwhile, we're bombarded with constant images of violence, greed, and fear that are desensitizing us and plunging us into a state of apathy. To escape, we surround ourselves with distractions. We look away from our own reality.

Outside, we're divided. Inside, we're fearful and fragmented. The present is a challenge, and we're anxious about the future.

We are told that our generation will not enjoy the same quality of life as our parents did. We are told that we are destroying nature. We are told to look at "the other" with suspicion.

Die-hard technology zealots even argue that the future of humanity has to be "transhuman." They tell us (in all seriousness) how we will soon be able to download our consciousness into computers and "let go of our humanity." "Dehumanization"—a word that was once similar to degradation and alienation—has now become a go-to fantasy for these technologists.

Yet, whether or not this nightmarish vision ever becomes a reality, we're at a point where we need to pause and seriously ask ourselves:

Is this what I'm looking for in my own life? Is this what I wish for my family and my friends? Is this what the great dream of humanity is really about?

You see, I believe we're not asking the right questions. Humanity has been growing by using the tools of science and technology—this is true. But, today, these tools are leading us to the brink of extinction. Why? Because humanity has not evolved as fast as its tools. Evolutionarily, we're still children playing with too much power.

  The answer we're looking for will not be found in more technology, but in rekindling our own humanity.

It's time for us to take a stand by choosing to evolve and experience the fullness of being human. This is done, individually, by daring to open the doors of our own creativity—and learn what its transformational power can really do. **Change comes from within.**

THE CREATIVE WAVE IS COMING
The genius inventor and visionary **R. Buckminster Fuller** (and one of my personal heroes) once told us, *"We are called to be architects of the future, not its victims."*

This is true.

We need to wake up. *Right now.*

And today, there's good news. It seems that many of us are instinctively realizing that it's time to reimagine the future and create something new.

There's a creative wave arising. Together, we're sharing a collective desire to dream, grow, and create positive change. And by bringing this desire into our own lives, each of us is contributing to this movement.

That's why I believe, my creative friend, that new experiences like the Creative Dreaming Method can be a great adventure for our generation *and* future generations. By taking a stand and saying, *"There's hope for our future—and I'm creating it today,"* we are becoming the agents of change who are bringing the new.

In fact (and this is what history has told us repeatedly), reality is nonlinear. Change doesn't follow a predictable curve. **Change comes in an instant.**

And change is up to all of us—regardless of our background, gender, age, or race. We know that the days when we kept hearing *"The experts are going to do it for us"* are over. Today, Life is calling each one of us (that means you) to step up and create the change we want to see in the world. Starting with our own lives. And in doing so, we will not only move collectively toward a positive future; we will evolve.

Here, you might think, but how? This is easier said than done—where do we start?

We start with you. We start right now.

My goal with the Creative Dreaming Method is to present you with a radical new map for transformation and possibility, a new perspective that will infuse you with an unstoppable desire to dream and create the life you want.

A life driven by hope, creativity, health, happiness, and meaning. A life where all the parts are moving together in unison. A beautiful life that you are meant to live. A life—balanced and whole—driven by community.

A life where we can all win, *together.*

This is why this book is designed in an unconventional way: mixing aphorisms, art, theory, practice, strategies, and conversations. The Creative Dreaming Method is meant to challenge you and to inspire you to imagine, create, and grow. But please, don't let the format distract you: My objective is for you to get actual results. I want to offer you a new kind of reading experience, as close as if we had spent a day together in a workshop—a long day ending in an evening conversation while we are looking at the stars. And if I did succeed, please say *"Hi,"* and let's continue this conversation.

I'd love to hear about your experience (you can find me online by visiting **ProfG.co**).

You see, my creative friend, we do live in complicated times. This is true. But we also live at an interesting turning point in history. Today is a moment when real change is ready to unfold.

And change begins with you. Change is in you. You are change.

Today, more than ever, your life—your journey—matters.

Enjoy this journey and start dreaming big dreams!
Dream with certainty.
Your life is waiting for you.

Shine on little star, shine on.
Let your light out.

      With love,
      Guillaume "Prof. G"

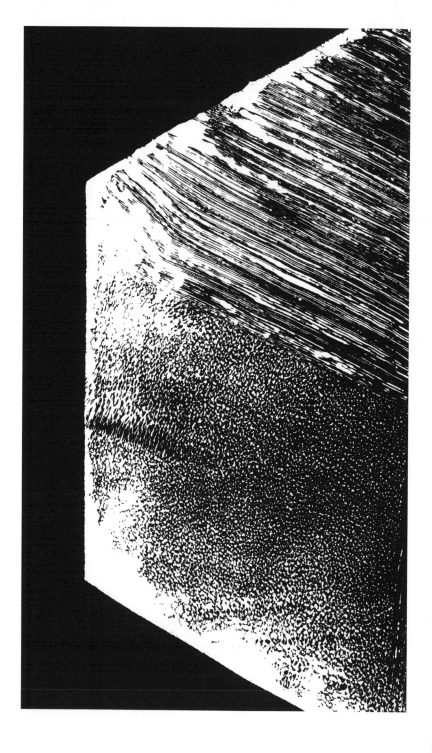

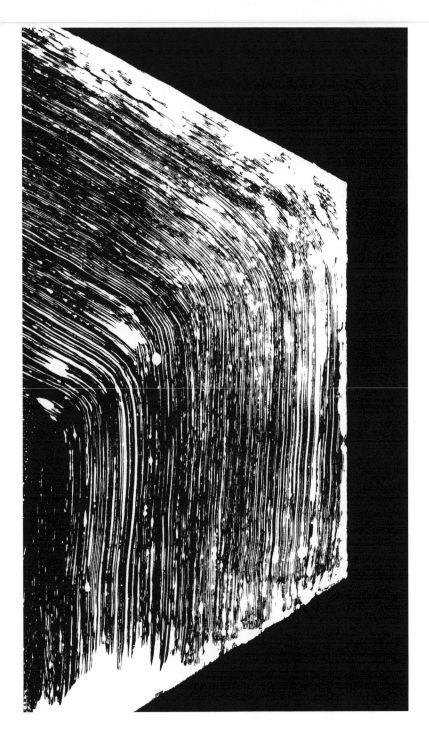

You can dream something beautiful
and make it real.

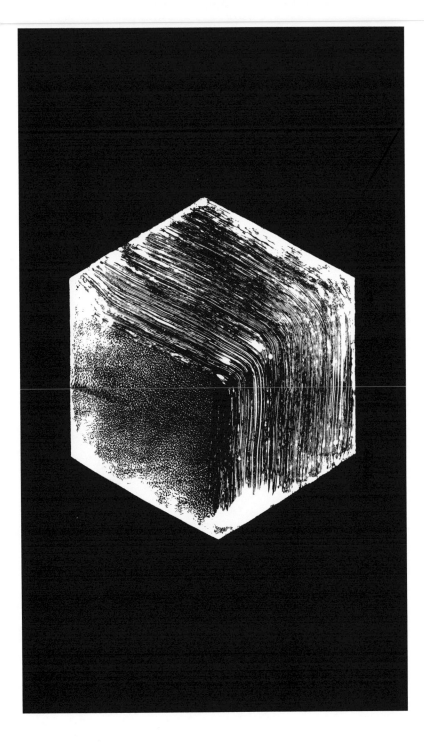

You're never too old or too young.
You're never too big or too small.
Just come as you are, today.

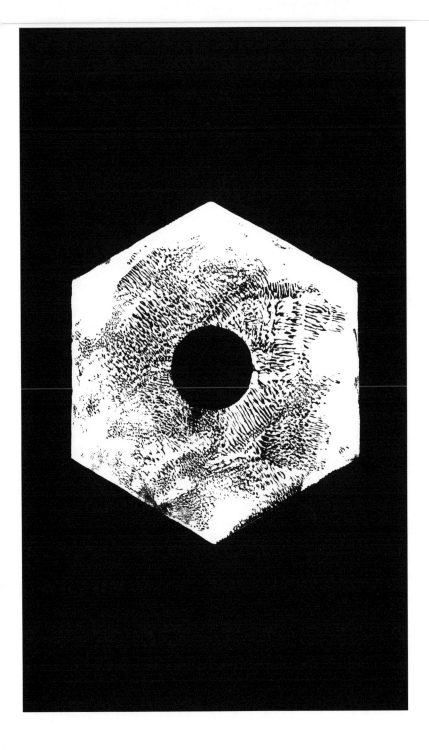

Take a stand by choosing to evolve and experience the fullness of being human.

Change comes from within.

When *you* create, *you* mutate.

Dream with certainty.

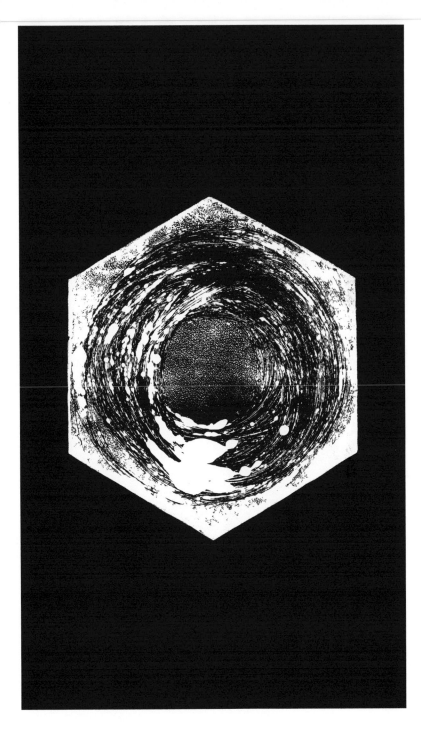

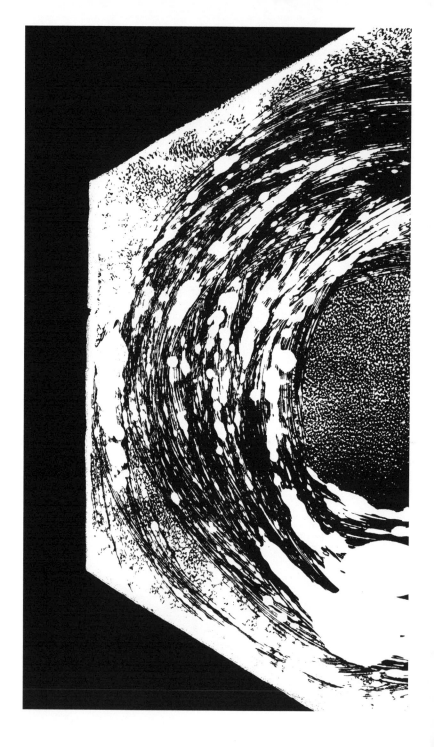

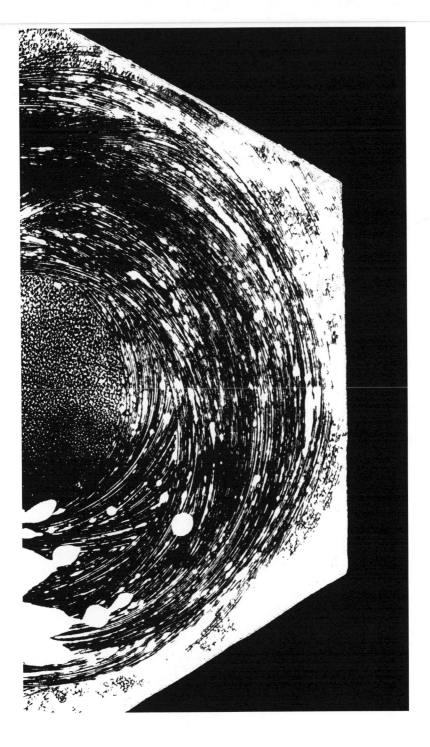

PART 1

THE BIG

PICTURE

WELCOME TO THE CREATIVE DREAMING METHOD

Hello, my creative friend. I hope that you are as excited as I am to get started. Let's begin with orientation—a short tour on how the Creative Dreaming Method works.

This book is created as a mini-workshop, and before we jump in, here are some pointers I'd like to share with you.

SEQUENCE
The Creative Dreaming Method follows a sequence. Unlike my previous books *You Are a Circle* and *You Are a Message*, which could be opened at any page, I'm inviting you to experience *You Are a Dream* from beginning to end. So please, if you have an urge to skip to the end, don't. This is because, in the Method, we're going through a process of discovery, meaning that the reading will take you step by step to a series of incremental insights.

The way I like to share the Creative Dreaming Method is to go from conceptual (big ideas) to tactical (practical applications)—which comes from my experience as a teacher. Over the years, I've found out that, in order to make a real impact, it's important to assimilate the key concepts first; then, we can go into the tactics.

A MODEL OF THE SELF
Our approach to individual change is inspired by the work of the anthropologist and philosopher **Gregory Bateson**. This model is represented as a dynamic sphere with several layers

expanding outward, from the center (inside) to the exterior (outside). It's simple; you can imagine it as an onion with multiple layers.

The **Model of the Self** (see Figure 1) works like this:

> Layer 0. **The core** (True Self)
> Layer 1. **Identity** (Persona)
> Layer 2. **Beliefs and Values**
> Layer 3. **Biology**
> Layer 4. **Skills and Behavior**
> Layer 5. **Environment**

The idea is that **everything in your life comes from the core** (Layer 0, and 1). And the way to create change outside is to work on the inside first. Once this is done, outside change comes naturally.

This is very important. Today, because we live in an age of top-ten lists and aggregated content, the vast majority of books and websites about creativity promote quick-fix strategies by attempting to change your skills and behavior (4), and environment (5) in order to get "fast results." While this approach claims to be very rational, it lacks potency. If you follow it, you'll either get temporary results with little impact, or more likely, it won't work at all.

In the Creative Dreaming Method, we are using a completely different strategy, with a unique focus on long-term, meaningful change.

Our approach to creativity and change comes from the core, with the understanding that it has an impact on everything else.

5   4   3   2   1   0

Fig. 1 - **The Model of the Self**
In the Creative Dreaming Method,
creativity and change originate from
the core.

Therefore, please make sure you first explore Part 1 and Part 2. And take some time to digest the content—there's no rush. The more you assimilate the core concepts, the faster you'll get meaningful results.

ENGAGEMENT

While you explore each part of the book and learn about the Creative Dreaming Method, I'd like to invite you to think about your own life and ask yourself:

"How can I use this? How can I experiment with that idea?"

Engagement is key. You can get incredible results with the Method if you integrate it within your own life. So please, have fun with it during our time together. Try doing small experiments. See how they work for you. My recommendation is that you read this book with a pen in hand. I've set up some space for you to write your notes/ideas in these pages—go for it.

Another way to be actively engaged in the reading is to discuss with a friend the passages from the book that resonate with you. Think about it as an open brainstorming session: Explore possibilities; see multiple directions your dream can take. Try small experiments. We use this approach with small groups in our workshops, and it's both fun and informative.

WHAT'S YOUR DREAM?

Finally, I'm also going to ask you to think about your dream— and make sure you hold that thought in your mind throughout our conversation.

You see, it's important to train your mind to imagine what can be possible for you. And here, you don't have to worry about the details. You've picked this book for a reason, haven't you? So go ahead: **Be bold. Dream big.**

Today, what's your dream?

And to help you out, I'll ask in a slightly different way:

Imagine we're five years from today . . . Imagine that what you've learned and implemented from this book has made a difference in your life.

● **Describe three meaningful dreams that you would be absolutely thrilled to realize in the next five years:**

1. _____

2. _____

3. _____

Wonderful. Now, please copy and write these down on a small card, and keep it in your wallet. And don't forget to put today's date on it. Look at the card on a regular basis to remind yourself that you are working on these dreams.

This card can be a very rewarding gift to your future self. Why? Because when you follow the Creative Dreaming Method, there's a high chance that you'll have grown so much in the next five years that you will not only have realized today's dreams, but you will have moved beyond them.

This just happened to me a few weeks ago. As I was cleaning up, I found one of these cards in an old wallet. And when

I reviewed my list, I noticed something strange . . . I was amazed to see that these goals and dreams were accomplished today—but in a better version than the ones I had originally envisioned. Everything was there, yet slightly brighter, bolder, and happier.

Try it—you'll surprise yourself.

And now that we're done with orientation, we're going to begin with the **10.10 Principles**, a series of ideas that will help us start our conversation.

THE 10.10 PRINCIPLES

The 10.10 Principles is a list of twenty concepts (10 About Life + 10 About You) that describe the world, from big to small. In the Creative Dreaming Method, these principles will serve as our backbone to create a map of reality and understand how the creative process works—on both a macro and micro level.

If you're reading this book for the first time and some of these principles seem a bit hard to grasp, don't worry. We're going to take the time to study and clarify them in the coming chapters.

I've decided to add them here at the beginning, so you can easily come back to them as you move forward into the book.

These principles are meant to inspire you. They are an invitation to reflect and to look at your life from a different perspective.

PART 1. ABOUT LIFE

Principle 1. The world we live in is a complex living system that contains an infinite number of complex living systems.

Principle 2. The universe is a complex living system.
Planet Earth is a complex living system.
The continent you live in is a complex living system.
Your country is a complex living system.
Your city is a complex living system.
Your neighborhood is a complex living system.
The company you work for (or your school)
is a complex living system.
Your friends and relationships are complex living systems.
Your family is a complex living system.
Your mind-body is a complex living system.
Your immune system is a complex living system.
Your cells are a complex living system.

Principle 3. Everything is interconnected.
From micro to macro, everything works together.
The small influences the big. The big influences the small.

Principle 4. Every complex living system only exists in relationship to the Whole. The Whole is made of the many. The many is a reflection of the Whole.

Principle 5. You are a relationship. You, your friends, your family, your school, your workplace, your city, your country and nature are all interconnected through an ongoing relationship. Nothing can exist long-term outside of it. Everything you see is the byproduct of a relationship existing within the Whole.

Principle 6. In this world, Life is the connective force that drives everything.
The universe is filled with living energy.
Everything in the world is either alive or participates in the process of Life.
Nothing exists outside of Life.

Principle 7. We know very little about Life.
We can't see it.
We can't measure it.
We can't create it.

Principle 8. All we can do is observe complex living systems, and based on our observations, refine our understanding of Life. We know that:

Life has agency (the capacity to act).
Life expands.
Life is an unfoldment.
Life is change.
Life follows cycles.
Life is adaptive.
Life perpetuates itself through an ongoing creative process.

Principle 9. Life's creative process follows this sequence:
Agency
Conception
Growth
Expansion & Replication
Dissolution

Principle 10. Complex living systems can be material (biological organisms and ecosystems): We call them Bio Systems.

Complex living systems can also be immaterial (concepts and ideas): We call them Idea Systems.

Some complex living systems (such as human beings) are both biological and ideational: We call them Bio-Idea Systems.

PART 2. ABOUT YOU
Principle 10.1. "You" are a consciousness living in a Bio-Idea System (your mind-body).

Principle 10.2. Every human being is the synthesis of Idea Systems (nurture, culture) and Bio Systems (biology) working together as one. You are both a biological and an ideation process. One cannot exist without the other. "You" would not exist without them.

Principle 10.3. As a Bio-Idea System, you are constantly evolving and changing. You are in relationship with—and the reflection of—Life's ongoing growth and creative process.

All you have is your process.
All you are is your process.

Principle 10.4. Life's creative process in your own being is always at work, even if you're not aware of it. By default, Life creates an automated Idea System in every individual: We call it the Persona. The Persona is a conditioned self (the product of nurture/culture). In many ways, the Persona can be compared to a computer virus. If the Persona is left unattended, it will take over your life by using mimicry (impersonating you).

Principle 10.5. In order to maintain its existence, the Persona encourages unawareness. The Persona's existence and action causes suffering because the Persona fears change and thrives on stagnation (status quo). By wanting to keep everything the same, the Persona acts in contradiction with life's natural cycle (change and growth).

Principle 10.6. The way to create true change in your life (Co-Evolution through growth) is a twofold process. It is done, first, by altering your Idea System and your Bio System through creative experiments. And next, by using the results of these creative experiments to dissolve the Persona and reclaim inner sovereignty.

Principle 10.7. The most effective way to dissolve the Persona is through the ongoing practice of actively raising awareness during creative experimentation (Creative Dreaming).

Principle 10.8. Creative Dreaming uses reality as a ground for process-based experimentation. Regardless of outcome, each creative experiment brings feedback, learning, and growth. Each creative experiment brings inner and outer transformation.

Principle 10.9. By Creative Dreaming, you are co-creating with the natural creative process of Life.

Principle 10.10. As a Creative Dreamer, you are creating the new, and altering reality. You are also experiencing the movement of your consciousness (True Self) arising.

CREATIVE POWER: THE HARD RESET

Now, my creative friend, let's start with a question:

How do you create change and growth?

In your own life, in business, or in our society—this is a very important question.

Think about it: To make your dream come true, any dream you can imagine for yourself must always be linked with your capacity to create change.

On a large scale, our capacity to adapt and constantly evolve by creating the new has helped humanity thrive and move forward. And every day, on a small individual scale, the same capacity helps us create a better life for ourselves and the people around us.

It doesn't matter what perspective (big or small) you decide to look at it from—creativity (or Creative Dreaming), is a critical, vital skill.

Unfortunately, today there are many misconceptions about what creativity or innovation means. Over the last two decades, "creativity" has slowly become a trendy buzzword—to the point of completely losing its original meaning.

The word "creative" has been co-opted in order to artificially boost the value of individuals or organizations. Listings for entry-level jobs are now asking for "creative thinkers." Titles such as "in-house visionary," "innovation guru," or "creativity ninja" are popping up inside some of the dullest companies. And finally, creativity/business conferences are blossoming everywhere with the promise of changing the world—one speech at a time. Inside these electrifying rallies, you'll find that everything suggests transformation, sometimes to the point of absurdity. For example, one memorable event I attended had its very own "Innovation Hub," which was actually the bar area.

None of this B.S. (this acronym standing, of course, for Boring Subterfuge) has anything to do with real creativity.

So, let's reset the clock, shall we? Here's what creativity is really about.

A creative act is revolutionary.
A creative act bends reality (what's commonly accepted as the norm), and redefines it.
A creative act is transformative.

As you can see, my creative friend, authentic creativity is a potent force that challenges the ordinary—it's not an empty buzzword. Creativity is a reality-altering power. Creativity brings deep change.

And it is under this framework that we're going talk about it in the Creative Dreaming Method.

THE CASE FOR THINKING ABOUT YOUR THINKING
Now, please imagine being at a dinner party and seeing a guest suddenly say, *"And now, let's think about our thinking!"*

No matter how charming, this burst of philosophical inquiry would probably fall flat. Why? Because, truthfully, no one likes to question their own thinking. Culturally, we are not very comfortable with challenging the accepted norm (the status quo).

Yet . . .

Creativity comes by approaching a problem from a completely new perspective. And the greatest creatives are all masters at using their minds differently.

In that sense, Creative Dreaming is connected with "thinking about thinking," and it calls for an inner transformation. To create the new, you need to move to a place that is beyond the limits of your habitual thinking patterns.

And there's more . . .

In order to move to this new place, you also need to evolve—because you cannot think differently without becoming a different person in the process. **By thinking like a new person, you're becoming a new person.**

Creativity is a twofold transformative power (both for individuals or organizations). And while in the context of this book I'm going to solely focus on the individual, the process is exactly the same for organizations. Real creativity is transformative—inside and outside.

Here, you may ask: *"Yes, but why change?"*

There are two scenarios that suggest the constant need for change.

One starts with a negative mindset that says, *"I (or we) can't do it!"* This disempowered stance, by denying the possibility for change, prevents any progress. So, here, change is obviously needed to create the new—and to create a renewed sense of empowerment.

The other is much more insidious. It's a positive tone that says, *"I'm [or we're] already successful, so why the need for change?"* Please note that this mindset also prevents any future progress. By using a "proven formula" for creative success that's entirely based on the past, it denies the present. This stance is actually very dangerous for both successful organizations and individuals. If this mindset becomes a habit, it always makes for spectacular falls.

Negative, or positive, both of these mindsets share a common thread: They stifle creativity and growth by trying to force a situation into "staying the same."

Both also presuppose an expected outcome (something we can predict already) based on a guess that uses past-centric knowledge/experience. This approach is called outcome-based thinking. It doesn't work because predicting the future based on the past is a fool's game.

So, no matter the scenario, the desire for things to stay the same (status quo) always creates stagnation. And in life, stagnation equals death (symbolic or literal).

Change is always needed: **Life is change** (see Principle 8). If you deny change, you will stop growing. If you stop growing, you will decay. This is always the case.

In contrast, the creative gesture not only brings in the new; it's also life affirming. **Through your own creative act, you are embodying Life's creative process.** In doing so, you are becoming more alive.

This is why the Creative Dreaming Method has two functions. First it's about creating change by bringing something new into the world. Second, the Method is a practice that will allow you to cultivate personal awareness and aliveness by being fully engaged with Life.

HOW TO DEFEAT RESISTANCE

I've shared with you that a true creative gesture is revolutionary. To bring in the new, you have to challenge the status quo. This always means that whenever you want to create, you will encounter friction. This friction can come in numerous shapes and forms, from within or without.

This is normal.

If you challenge reality in order to alter it, it will push back. And the more innovative your ideas, the more friction you will get. This is why many talented creatives—with great ideas—end up giving up. The level of resistance they face is simply too much to handle.

So how do you make resistance go away? Here's a brutal answer: You can't. It will always be there. Reality, to be real, is resistance.

Reality resists!

But . . .

When it comes to the Creative Dreaming Method, there's a key element you need to know.

By changing how you perceive (and how you interact with) reality, resistance is redefined and loses its potency because it's now part of your process.

The more you master the method to create change, the more you change. And the more you change, the easier it gets for you to go around obstacles.

This new perspective—based on inner transformation—is what we'll discuss during our time together.

HOW DO I KNOW THIS? WHY IT WORKS

Now, my creative friend, I'd like to go into what authentic creativity is, in the everyday. But before I do so, I'd like to share with you where I got these ideas from. Here's the backstory . . .

As mentioned before, I have a peculiar background: I'm mostly self-taught (with the help of great mentors). So in order to figure things out, I've studied creativity all my life. I've been learning about this subject obsessively for over three decades, and I'm still doing it to this day.

As part of this search, I dedicated eight years of my life to working as creative director of an art and design magazine—to deepen my inquiry by going straight to the source. In that time, I had the incredible opportunity to meet and conduct interviews with some of the best creatives on the planet in every creative category: art, design, fashion, architecture, music, craft, and business.

And here's what I've discovered. All the world-class creative visionaries have one thing in common: They are driven by their creative process.

In fact, they are obsessed with it. And it is this very focus that allows them to move beyond any setbacks.

These people are the greatest in their categories because they constantly challenge themselves to grow—they never stop innovating. Inwardly and outwardly, they are looking to push themselves beyond what's expected.

Creative visionaries are involved in an ongoing dialogue between life, themselves, and reality. They constantly refine their creative gesture—which forces them to grow. They are constantly evolving.

To quote the designer extraordinaire **Philippe Starck** (whom I had the pleasure of interviewing), this evolution is akin to a mutation. *"We all are mutants,"* Starck told me. *"Let's accept being mutants, let's enjoy being mutants, let's consciously manage our mutation"* (*Whitewall* Magazine, Issue 16).

Quite an interesting or provocative statement, isn't it?

Yet this uncommon idea is actually the norm with all the top creatives I've encountered. All are involved in growing (or mutating) outside and inside, simultaneously.

You see, the real creative practice is an ongoing outer and inner transformation process.

AUTHENTIC CREATIVITY IS PROCESS-BASED

To imagine the future and create the new, it's key that you first get to a space of "unknowing."

In the Creative Dreaming Method, "unknowing" means creating a space of possibilities (even if these possibilities are just tiny seeds of an idea), rather than trying to guess or predict what the future can be like.

This is done by allowing the process of creative discovery to reveal what's possible—even if this process may involve temporary setbacks. Creative Dreamers adopt a "beginner's mind" entirely focused on the potential of the present. This approach is called process-based thinking. And process-based thinking (and acting) fosters innovation.

But concretely, what does it mean for you?

As a Creative Dreamer, when you're process-based, you are entirely focused on your creative process. This means that **everything in your life is organized around the idea of growth**, one day at a time.

Everything.

You are only interested in what you're doing right now (not the successes/failures of the past or the hopes/fears of an imaginary future). Everything is about what you are doing *now*—your process. This involves, of course, continuously pushing yourself outside of your comfort zone in order to grow.

At the end of each day, you ask yourself: *"How well did I work today? Did I push myself? Did I try something new?"*

And if you can answer *"yes,"* every single day, then you're on the right track.

But there's more . . . Because, here, my creative friend, there's a major twist. The process-based approach implies the accomplishment of an incredible feat.

For your creative greatness to unfold, you need to evolve into a new you. The "mutation" that Philippe Starck talks about actually needs to occur.

Getting outside of the limitations of your own mind calls for a real change. No change is possible on the outside if you don't change on the inside as well.

How does it work?

For this transformation to happen, you must first be daring enough to ask a very big question.

And this question is so big that it's the ultimate transformative question.

This is where our journey of the Creative Dreaming Method really begins . . .

Together, we're going to enter uncharted territory.

Get ready for a wild ride.

WHO ARE YOU? THE BIG QUESTION
To become a Creative Dreamer who can bring about change, you need to discover how Life's creative process operates at the individual level. And first, you must be fully aware of how this process works in your own life. Together, we're going to put on our "philosopher's hat" and inquire about this relationship between you and reality.

So let's get to it, and let me ask you the big question:

Who are you?

You see, my creative friend, for thousands of years, since Ancient Egypt and, later Greece, this question has preoccupied humanity. Yet, today, it still remains a collective mystery. It's an impenetrable riddle whose answer has only revealed itself to a few daring souls.

Why is that?

The mystery is proportionate to the reward.

Solving the mystery of self-knowledge is no less than the key to ultimate freedom.

It's the discovery that can allow us to move from a half-asleep state into becoming what **Abraham Maslow** has called the fully aware, "self-actualized" individual. Or, in our case, the Creative Dreamer.

Yet, even after thousands of years of cultural legacy, true self-realization remains an elusive process. The reason for this is that Life has created a series of "locks" that are preventing us from inquiring into the subject to begin with. Knowledge of the True Self is a guarded realm.

"Guarded by whom?" you may ask. Well, . . . a classic story comes to mind.

In *The Republic*, the Greek philosopher **Plato** masterfully describes in "The Allegory of the Cave" how we all are prisoners of our own perceptions. In this story, he shows that what we call reality is just a box we live in—a prison we're born into. In this prison/cave, we are looking at a screen, watching a projection of shadows (just like in a movie theater), and we mistakenly believe it's the real thing.

Plato suggests that even if a prisoner were to escape and discover what was really happening outside the prison's walls he would, upon his return, be met with rejection by the remaining prisoners. They would not believe him.

According to Plato, it appears that we love our delusions more than reality.

This idea that the reality we perceive is but a speck of a larger whole is not limited to ancient Greece. It's shared by many cultures and ancient traditions. For example, it's a key concept in Eastern thought, where reality is called "**Maya**," a Sanskrit word that means "appearance," "illusion," "trick," or "magic." We also find it under a different guise in all shamanic cultures where dreams, or the dream world, coexist side-by-side and interact with physical reality.

Curiously, men and women of science also recognize this idea. **David Bohm**, one of the most important theoretical physicists and creative minds of the twentieth century, has suggested something similar with his mathematical and physical theory of "implicate" and "explicate" order. And today, many contemporary quantum physicists commonly state that what we call reality (or observer-driven reality) is just one aspect of a much larger, interconnected system/whole.

But if ancient philosophers and modern scientists are essentially saying the same thing, why isn't this idea a part of basic human knowledge?

As mentioned before, this knowledge is a guarded realm.

When it comes to self-knowledge and our understanding of the nature of reality, Life is playing one major "trick" on all of us.

And guess what? . . . Like every great magic show, the "trick" works because we are unaware it exists.

We are completely unaware that we are living in our reality box (Plato's cave-prison)—not just because we're absorbed in it through our senses, but because *we* are the box.

LEARN COSMIC HUMOR FIRST
So, my creative friend, before we go down the rabbit hole (because that's where we're about to go), and to prep this conversation properly, I'd like to frame it in a way that's healthy, straightforward, and nonthreatening.

And here, I'd like to ask you:
Can you have a sense of humor when it comes to your sense of self?

If you slip and fall into a pile of mud, can you laugh about it?

If you make a social faux pas, can you laugh it off?

If during a romantic picnic date, bird poop lands on your head, can you playfully say, *"This terrible B.S. (or Bird Surprise) is a happy sign of destiny,"* then clean up and happily move on to enjoy your day?

I hope you can answer "yes" to these questions.

This is very important. While I've only been presenting insignificant little moments (don't ever let a little bird ruin your day), humor is actually key for creativity, health, and happiness. Human life can often be a challenging and complicated affair, and humor acts as a protection mechanism. It's an inner fire that will always bring back hope in any situation.

In the Creative Dreaming Method, humor is the cure for desperation and the vehicle through hardships. And your capacity to elegantly plow through hardships is directly related to your level of creative success.

Here, of course, I'm not talking about being goofy or ironic. I suggest that you adapt to cosmic humor by recognizing that Life is a play that constantly challenges you to find grace—and embody grace—in the most ungraceful moments. These are the moments when there's (apparently) no more hope—these are Life's cosmic jokes. And yes, from an individual perspective, they can be extremely brutal.

For you, when confronted with Life's greatest challenges, this would mean taking a stand by saying that you're ready to play full on.

"Okay, Life! There's no more hope—I get the joke—I've lost, you win. But watch me . . . Watch me create hope, no matter what. Watch me grow and evolve. Watch me never stop trying and refining my approach until change comes about. Watch me do this for years, watch me do this every day for the rest of my life, as long as I have a pulse."

My creative friend, what I just wrote might not be your style, and that's fine. Feel free to adapt it and rephrase it the way you want. Or don't rephrase it—simply feel it.

What's important here is not the form or style you choose to adopt; what counts is the humorous resolve.

In the Creative Dreaming Method, we call this playful attitude the "**defiant stance**."

The defiant stance is powerful. By challenging Life—and any obstacles she can (and will) throw at you—you move away from acting out a stress-response; and instead, you begin using creative play and problem solving. Humor gives you the critical distance you need to succeed in finding innovative solutions.

This is essential in the Creative Dreaming Method.

This approach works against the greatest challenges Life has to offer. Recognize the humor of an impossible situation and defiantly decide—by finding the resolve within yourself—to become the unstoppable force that will bring about change.

Do it playfully.

Now that we've agreed that a healthy dose of humor can help

us thrive, please pack it up and bring it along as we continue in this journey to find the Self.

We're ready to start.

YOU ARE A RELATIONSHIP

The search for the Self is shaped like a very intricate labyrinth.

Previously, I wrote:

*"We are unaware that we are living in a box—not just because we're absorbed in it through our senses—but because **we are the box.**"*

What do I mean by that? How did this box come about?

One of the fundamental principles of the Creative Dreaming Method is that we, human beings, are "living systems" (See Principle 2). It simply means that we are never isolated because we are a part of a larger whole (family, friends, society, nature, etc.). Therefore, **we are always the byproduct of a series of relationships** (direct or indirect).

You are here, today, because of these relationships. And these relationships are an expression of Life's ongoing creative process.

You exist because of Life's creative play. "You" are a relationship.

Please take a moment to think about this . . .

Imagine and track back to the origins of your life—as far as you can take it. And think about what had to happen (worldwide, throughout history) for you to be here, at this very moment.

Really think about it . . . Trillions upon trillions of interconnected events have had to happen for you to be here.

Your existence is nothing short of a miracle. And everything in life has, in a way, participated in it.

You have been created, not just by your parents, but by your ancestors and the entire human adventure. You have been created by Life itself.

Isn't it incredible?

You see, most of the time, we're **unaware** of this process because it's beyond our immediate experience. The word "unaware" is very important in our conversation. Our lack of awareness means that we are asleep to some of the most vital aspects of our lives.

But this gets even more interesting . . .

Because you exist as part of a larger dynamic of relationships, everything you see, think, or do is directly influenced by this process. This process is at work in your life today.

This ongoing creative process (that you are) simultaneously defines both your "self" and how you see "reality" (more on this later).

Let's go back to Plato's story . . . We can now start to understand why the prison he was describing in the "Allegory of the Cave" is so airtight.

In this context, the deep interconnectedness between you and Life also implies a darker side: By defining and being both your "self" and your "reality," it creates a limited perceptive wall around you—that's the prison Plato was describing. **And you can't escape from a prison when "you" are the prison—and when the prison defines who you think you are.**

In other words, what you see and feel (your sense of self, your sense of reality) is directly influenced by an infinite number of relationships and influences that prevent you from seeing the big picture. This is Plato's prison, and we're all born into it.

Pretty intense, isn't it?
Let me illustrate this with a story.

Let's imagine going together to a well-known tourist spot in California: the Santa Monica Pier. You'll find beachside stores, food, games, and a Ferris wheel. In this story, the pier represents our reality. Let's look at the crowd and pick different characters, all experiencing this reality differently.

- A young child: For her, the pier is all about fun and adventure—playing, eating cotton candy, and finding the courage to ride on the Ferris wheel.
- The pier director and his team: For them, this is hard work and problem solving. They want everything to runs smoothly, and their job is to make sure it will.
- The pickpocket: For him, the pier is an opportunity to make quick cash while trying not to get caught.
- The police officer: For him, it's all about making sure he'll catch the pickpocket who is ruining the tourists' experience.

As you can see, this is the same reality, yet everyone perceives it differently. And each character will argue that their view of the pier (what they know about it) is the correct one.

The process is the same on a larger scale. We all see the world differently because of our internal representation of who we are, and what reality is.

We are trapped in our reality box.
We don't see reality as it is, but as we are.
We are—and live inside—a reality/self.

So now, my creative friend, you may ask . . .

"Is there a way out?"

Fortunately, yes, there is.

Despite the odds (which may seem to be against us), we all possess many gifts, and we need to learn how to use them.

We all come equipped with: an infinite imagination, a sense of observation, self-reflective awareness (the capacity for introspection, being able to watch the movements of our own thought), and, of course, creativity.

This is great news. Together, these are the tools we're going to learn in order to open the doors of Plato's Cave and create change.

But before we start, we must first understand our "self."

How is it created? How does the self appear and sustain itself?

The creation of the self you call "you" takes place on two fronts simultaneously: psychological (or more precisely, in our conversation: ideational) and physical.

Together, we'll start with the creation of the mysterious Persona (ideational creation of the self); and next, we'll move into the creative process connected with the physical body.

PERSONAL CREATION STORY AND THE PERSONA
How do you become "you," my creative friend?

As we just discovered, you exist as part of a large-scale creative process. "You" are a relationship.

Now let's find out, concretely, how it all begins . . .

You were born in a specific context (family), in a specific culture. And this context was driven by a **Personal Creation Story**, a cultural narrative that was passed onto you. It could be a good thing or a bad thing—and for most of us, it was probably a little bit of both.

For example, in my family, I heard many stories growing up. We had the "gentleman farmer" story, about an ancestor who had nine farms in the Loiret region of France and who also had nine children. Next, there was the story of World War II—no food, and many other hardships. Next, there was life in West Africa (where I was born), and what it was like living there. Some of these stories were beautiful and inspiring; others were negative and depressing. These stories talked about what life and people were about: They created a map of the shared "reality" my family considered important.

This Creation Story does not happen in your life overnight. As a child, you went through years of conditioning to learn how to be "you." This conditioning was applied and reinforced by parental figures, teachers, school friends, television, advertising, and social media, who repeatedly told you who you were (or weren't); what was expected of you (or not); and what was possible in your life (or not).

Please note, my creative friend, that in many ways, this ongoing Creation Story process (it's still happening every day) defines how you see yourself, and how you see the world.

In sociology, this process is called enculturation. It's actually vital for a child's well-being because it's impossible to develop a healthy biology and/or psychology without this cultural input (see Principle 10.2).

The relationship between your biology and the stories/ideas that were (and are) shared with you is what makes you a human being. This ongoing process in your mind-body forms a Bio-Idea System.

It may sound funny to put it like that, but you and I are both Bio-Idea Systems.

Unfortunately, this process comes with some strings attached. Shockingly, it doesn't always support your well-being.

To begin with, your Personal Creation Story is always enforced through a reward/punishment conditioning. And as a child, you had very little say about it. And because this process is ongoing (and continues to this day), it restricts your capacity for freedom.

The **Personal Creation Story** accomplishes several things. First, it directly shapes your **sense of self** (where all your thoughts about yourself and the world come from). Next, it also implies your **social positioning in society**, and that also defines your capacity to see "reality" (your **reality box**). In addition—because it runs on automatic (without your input)—this process also creates a conditioned "self," which we call, in the Creative Dreaming Method, the **Persona**. And then, the Persona reinforces the Personal Creation Story.

Now, combine these together and you have a formula that works like a loop:

⋯▶ **Personal Creation Story = sense of self + social positioning = reality box = Persona** ⋯

As you can see, this process is very mechanical. The byproduct of your Personal Creation Story is not so much the true, independent Self you'd expect to find, but an artificial image, the **Persona**.

Your Persona (the social self that reflects your Personal Creation Story passed onto you) works automatically. It thinks for you, it dreams for you, it craves for you, and so on. It's the part of you that automatically says, for example: *"In our family, we always love/hate _____ [fill in the blank]."* And of course, without any real explanation for why this is so and/or why this cannot be changed.

Now, here's the really scary part. This is not only bizarre; it works!

The more you conform to the Personal Creation Story and

believe you actually are your Persona, the more you'll find confirmation of its validity in the world around you. An inner/outer reality creation loop is being generated, following a simple process.

From your perspective, it works like something like this:

> 1. The Personal Creation Story I was born into creates my conditioned sense of self (Persona).
> 2. My Persona creates my social positioning in society.
> 3. My social positioning in society creates my mode of thinking.
> 4. My mode of thinking creates how I see reality (my reality box).
> 5. And now, how I see and interpret reality always confirms and reinforces my Personal Creation Story—repeat!

This mechanism creates a perfect vicious circle that feeds upon itself. Interestingly, the loop works both ways—even if you try running away from it!

For example, let's pretend that you've discovered (maybe by reading this book) this awful Persona loop and decide to escape from it. Here's what happens:

> 1. If you rebel, and decide to move away from your original Creation Story, you're therefore creating and conforming to a new image, a new Story you're fabricating called "I'm a rebel."
> 2. The new Story creates your sense of self (a new Persona called "I'm a rebel").
> 3. Your new Persona creates your social positioning in society.

4. Your social positioning in society creates your mode of thinking.

5. Your mode of thinking creates how you see reality (your reality box). And now, how you see and interpret reality always confirms and reinforces your new Personal Creation Story—repeat!

(Please make sure you catch this amusing "rebel paradox": By rebelling against "something," what you create can only exist in relationship to the very "thing" you're rebelling against to begin with. There's no real change—just moving to the other side of the same coin.)

The Persona and the Quest for the True Self

As you can imagine, on an individual level, to actually realize and see clearly how this mechanism operates is not easy.

First, we are culturally conditioned to accept without question that the Persona is who we are. Therefore, we rarely question what it says.

As an example, I've heard a million times this sentence, growing up in Paris, France: *"Me, I'm French. And we, the French, value good food/life/conversation/art/quality of life/music/culture/literature/philosophy_____ (here, fill in the blank with any template statement)"* [*"Moi, j'suis Français. Et nous, en France, on apprécie la bonne _____ "*]. And whatever came out from these generalizations was always accepted as being true—even when these statements were completely false.

I'm sure you've heard similar things in your life as well.

And these generalizations also imply behaviors or what is considered to be normal. Here, let me stay with the Parisian life as an example.

You might be surprised to learn that there are stores in Paris where you can buy a box of artisanal chocolates that retail for $100. For some French people, this is considered "normal" because these (truly amazing) chocolates are part of the *savoir vivre* (art of living) tradition. And by looking at it this way, they connect these chocolates with their Personal Creation Story. These chocolates become a part of their identity—their Persona.

Now, you could wonder, *"Is this really 'normal'?"*

It all depends on who's asking the question. Very few people around the world would be willing to pay this price for chocolates—because culturally, it doesn't make any sense for them. But, again, for some French people (not all), it's indeed considered "normal."

And now let's go to the U.S.: Is it normal to pay $1,000 (or more) for a pair of sneakers? It all depends who you're talking to. Some sneakerheads would agree that it's completely rational, indeed, to "invest" thousands in a specific brand.

You see, your culture creates your Persona, an automatic self that constantly tells you what is acceptable, or not. What's normal, or not. What's real, or not. The Persona thinks for you.

On a personal level, we have a hard time spotting the Persona at work in our own lives. The reason is simple. The Persona is really good at hiding—its existence depends on it.

The Persona's sole goal is to survive. To do so, it makes us believe it is us by using mimicry, impersonating us—yes, the Persona is that weird little voice that you can catch, once in a while.

When the Persona wants you down, instead of saying, *"You always suck at this,"* it says, *"I always suck at this."* When the Persona wants you to overeat, instead of saying, *"You need this dessert,"* it screams instead, *"I want it!"*—and here, if you've ever had a craving for a specific type of food, you know exactly what I'm talking about. Your mind is being hacked.

Using the "I" allows the Persona to make you believe it's "you."

And when you combine both forces together (Persona and Personal Creation Story), we are overpowered. We are more likely to mistake the Persona for our True Self.

THE QUEST BEGINS
My creative friend, as you can imagine, the concept of the Persona is too radical for most people to accept.

The slight suggestion that, maybe, what we think, feel, and react to might be the byproduct of multiple dynamic cultural systems and conditioned patterns running on automatic . . . simply sounds too daunting!

And it is.

But let me ask you this: Thinking about the way I am describing the Persona, can you call to mind people you know who are just like that? People entirely driven by ideas they've received from outside sources? People who act in almost robotic ways because their culture tells them it's the right thing to do?

I'm sure you can.

The concept of the Persona is not only radical, it's also full of scary implications. Once you know how to spot it, you begin to see it everywhere.

But while it's easy to spot it in others, it's harder to recognize it in ourselves.

After all, we all believe we are masters of our own lives. Independent thinkers. Are we not?

You see, this is a scary idea. And that's why we need a sense of humor when discussing the self.

Yet, the quest for ultimate freedom and expression begins by unveiling and confronting the Persona.

In the Creative Dreaming Method, understanding how the Persona operates is the key to our creative map of reality. It brings complete clarity about how life works, both on a micro (you) and macro level (society). It clarifies why we are faced with so many problems individually and collectively—and more importantly (as we'll discover later on), it also shows us how we can solve them.

YOUR PERSONA IS NOT YOUR FRIEND

As we discovered, the Personal Creation Story, when unchal-lenged, invariably creates a Persona. The Persona is a kind of automated fake-self (similar to what Zen Buddhism refers to as the Ego Self) that we mistakenly believe to be our own true identity, our True Self. For this to happen, the Persona uses mimicry as a hiding mechanism. It impersonates us by speaking on our behalf, using our own voice.

The Persona is easy to spot. It's that weird little voice that comments on every aspect of your life (often, in a very negative, judgmental tone): *"I've never been good enough for this"*; *"I can't change."* Or sometimes, it's the triumphant (and delusional) version that sounds like this: *"I'm always right! Everyone else is an idiot!"* And the classic: *"I'm fine like this. I don't want to change anything!"*

What's wrong with the Persona? You may ask.

Everything.

You see, the Persona is not your friend.

THE PERSONA IS LIKE A COMPUTER VIRUS
Because it's automatic and autonomous, the Persona's only concern is self-survival—at all cost. The Persona's survival is paradoxically completely unrelated to *your* own well-being. In order to exist, the Persona needs to be absolutely "right," even if this means that you'll die spiritually, emotionally, or physically in the process.

To give you an analogy from the computer world, the Persona is a little bit like software that's only interested in self-preservation, regardless of consequences. In computer science, this type of software is called a **virus**: a self-replicating computer program which installs itself without user consent. That's your Persona.

The Persona manifests itself in the darkest, ugliest, and saddest human behaviors:

> • The husband who physically abuses his wife because he's *"right."*
> • The alcoholic who drinks himself to death because he's *"not corrupted, like everyone else."*
> • The religious fanatic who kills another man—and himself—because he's *"on a mission for God."*
> • The businessman who sells a product that actually destroys the physical health of his customers (or nature), and reassures himself by saying he has *"bills to pay and a family to take care of."*
> • The tourist who drops trash wherever he/she goes because *"someone else will pick it up."*
> • The parent who *"beats some sense"* into his/her child because he/she *"was raised this way."*
> • The creative who gives up on her art because she's *"not good enough, and it's too risky."*
> • The intelligent soul who never dares to speak up because *"speaking up gets you in trouble."*
> • The workaholic who neglects his family because *"this is the price of success."*

The list is infinite, and you can see it everywhere. You and I have seen the Persona before, unfortunately, way too many times.

THE PERSONA LIVES IN THE PAST AND CANNOT CREATE

Any way you look at it, the Persona always brings pain because, at its roots, it's always based on fear.

The Persona's greatest fear is the fear of change—and creativity is change. Change is the greatest enemy of the Persona because authentic change automatically dissolves it.

This is extremely important to understand: Because the Persona cannot create something new (change, a project, or an experience), it will do anything it can to try to sabotage your creative efforts.

The Persona is past-centric, and it will relentlessly ask you to stay the same—suggesting that the only way to survive is to repeat or duplicate known situations from the past.

This means that the individual who is entirely driven by his or her Persona is equipped with a robotic one-track mind whose only goal is preserving the status quo (things as they are) by avoiding change.

The Persona always wants a known outcome based on past experience. The Persona is morbidly rigid. It lives only in the past and never wants to create something new, because if it does, the Persona has to change—which it can't do, or it will "die." **Creativity or change means death for the Persona.**

THE PERSONA ALWAYS WANTS TO BE RIGHT
The Persona is constantly looking for outside validation that the Personal Creation Story (which created it in the first place) is always correct. Therefore, the Persona needs to be "absolutely right" all the time.

To survive, the Persona must deny change and/or reality by making the host (you) remain unaware in order to make sure that you will not question anything the Persona does or says.

Everything will be put aside by the Persona in order to survive and be "right." To exist, it will deny your needs, aspirations, self-expression, independent thinking, self-love, innovation, growth, sense of being connected to the whole, even love.

Everything that's good for your soul, the Persona will deny.

As a result, a human being solely driven by his or her Persona will be disconnected, regressive, angry, frozen, repressed, fearful, robotic. And through denial and repression he or she will "go unaware" at every opportunity. Meaning that the individual will stack up behaviors that will keep him or her in a state of permanent unawareness—becoming asleep while awake.

THE PERSONA'S FAVORITE TOOL IS UNAWARENESS

How do you identify the Persona in yourself? It's easy.

You can see the Persona at work by observing how it gently "invites you" into unawareness.

After mimicry, unawareness is the second trick the Persona uses to keep you bound to it. It makes you unaware of its action by making you blank out, giving you a mental block, or overriding you with a strong emotion (such as fear, desire, or anger). Once the emotion takes over, unawareness rises up.

In daily life, unawareness manifests itself through multiple behaviors, from the extreme to the mundane: drug/alcohol use; violence; overeating; depression; addiction to entertainment; addiction to shopping; addiction to sex; addiction to gambling; self-absorption; constant daydreaming; regression into fantasy;

addiction to social media; compulsive house cleaning, and so on. The list is infinitely long, and it's not a good list.

The Persona's favorite tool is unawareness because while the host (that's you) is unconscious, the Persona can take over. We will discuss in **Part 2 Obstacles** how this process operates (and how to defeat it).

And in time, the more the Persona takes over, the more it is difficult for the host to realize that it has been under its constant influence to begin with. That's the perfect trap.

Individually and collectively, the Persona is the plight of humanity—a jail. Like Plato's Cave, it defines who we think we are, and how we perceive reality.

The vast majority of the population lives asleep—in a state of unawareness. Every day, billions of humans go about their lives in a permanent daze, like daylight sleepwalkers. Sometimes, in brief moments, they wonder why life seems to "happen" to them . . . But finding no answer they go back to living a Persona-governed life—entirely based on the past, mechanical—a life filled with unhappiness, frustration, and of course . . . unawareness.

The Persona and the process of unawareness is what prevents us from living an authentic creative life. By being bound to the past, we can never experience the gift of the present.

As you can see, the Persona is not your friend.

IS THIS REALLY YOU?

Here, my creative friend, I'd like to invite you to take a really deep breath (and I'm doing it, too, as I write this!).

This talk about Persona is not the easiest. I know it can be a bit uncomfortable if you've never considered this idea before. But—before you go unaware by closing this book and throwing it at the wall, please tell your Persona to chill for a second.

Let's hang together for a little longer, shall we?

Because the good stuff is coming (it is).

What I just described is tough. And it's exactly what Plato was talking about in the Allegory of the Cave. And guess what: By just reading this passage about the Persona, you are now more aware than 90 percent of the human population.

Congrats, my creative friend!

And, by the way, let's not make this more dramatic than what it really is. It doesn't really matter what your Persona looks like today, because life is change.

It's okay; we're all here to grow.

Because there's something more important here . . . The real question is:

Is this really you?

You see, when you look at something in your life that's limiting, or controlling you—for example, a voice that says, *"I'm *not good enough"* or *"This can't be done"* or *"Everything must be perfect!"*

Simply start by asking yourself: *"Is this really me?"*

Bring full awareness to what you're thinking, doing, or feeling. Be there 100 percent.

Because you see, **awareness is the key**. It's the killer of the Persona. In order to reconnect with the True Self and answer the age-old question *"Who Am I?"* awareness is your first step to self-discovery.

The more you practice awareness, the more your True Self unfolds.

● **Exercise: Self-Reflective Awareness Experiment**
Now, let's try together this simple exercise. An easy, five-minute meditation on your Persona. It's really simple. Ask yourself this one question:

— Am I my job?

And here, don't skip this exercise; please, actually do it. Close your eyes, if it helps. And if you want, you can take a deep breath. Simply, ask yourself:

— Am I my job?

The goal of the exercise is to observe whatever thought comes up. Just observe your thoughts without judgment (the good, the bad, and the funny). See what comes up . . . Your only goal is to relax and place yourself in the observer position. Please try this for five minutes. Start now.

. . .

Welcome back.

So what happened? What thoughts came about? Did you stay on track or did your Persona suddenly take over and start saying weird things like:

> *"I thought this was a book about Creative Dreaming— what's this Persona nonsense!"*

> *"I'm hungry. I wonder what's in the fridge?"*

> *"Of course, I'm not my job! This is ridiculous!"*

> *"Of course, I am my job! This is ridiculous!"*

> *"The neighbors' dog is really driving me mad. Why can't he stop barking?"*

> *"Man, I'm bored. I wonder if they're releasing a new episode of my favorite show tonight?"*

> *"Do I need to buy toothpaste today, or is there enough left for one last brush?"*

If you've spotted any curious thoughts popping up during this exercise, congrats—you've just met with your Persona.

Wait! What? . . . You did not do this exercise because, *"This is stupid! I can skip this and do it later!"*

Well, well, well . . . congrats, my creative friend—you've just met with your Persona! (Did I get you there?)

This type of meditation exercise is called self-reflective awareness—which simply means your capacity to observe your own thoughts. This is a common meditation practice that's very useful to uncover the Persona and see it at work.

The key with the self-reflective awareness technique is never to judge the thoughts that come up. The classic advice is to look at them "like passing clouds" or "like dogs running in a yard." You just let them be.

The idea is to get into the habit of contemplating your own thoughts by placing yourself in the position of an observer. Here's why it works: Obviously, when you observe something, you can't simultaneously be "it."

● **Exercise: Daily Practice: Is This Really Me?**
In the Creative Dreaming Method, self-awareness plays a really big role. A good habit is to look at your thought process—judgment-free.

When you're in your car, stuck in traffic, traveling, or listening to a boring lecture by an uninspiring teacher (yes, students, I feel your pain), you might notice that your thoughts will run on automatic. You will start daydreaming or commenting automatically on the situation.

When you catch one of these automatic thoughts, ask yourself:

"Is this really me?"

Here, you're not looking for an answer but connecting with the experience of the present moment. You are taking the position of the observer—that's all.

After you are used to this practice for a while, the next step is to bring it up when you get overwhelmed by a negative emotion. This is harder.

Let me give you an example. Let's pretend a driver cuts you off on the road and you start swearing at him (in your head, or verbally). Really observe what this voice is truly saying, and ask:

> *"Is this really me?"*

This exercise is a great way to reveal and get to know your Persona. And every time you're taken over by a negative emotion such as anger, fear, or boredom, or when you catch yourself being in state of unawareness, use the same approach, and observe your thoughts.

> Again, ask yourself: *"Is this really me?"*

If you practice this self-reflective exercise for a while, you will discover that many of your thoughts are randomly generated, as if you had no control over them. You might also notice that these thoughts might sound very judgmental or even cruel. You might be really surprised by how graphic they can be. Don't panic; it doesn't mean that you are a bad person. In fact, refrain from judging these thoughts. Simply look at them from an observer's perspective, and let them go.

The more you practice, the less power these thoughts will have.

While this is a really brief introduction to the practice of self-reflective awareness, this exercise is very potent and transformative because it uncovers the Persona.

You can experiment with it whenever "a weird little voice pops in." Become the observer of your own thoughts. Or perhaps I should say: Become the observer, and watch your Persona reacting.

And to answer our original question: *"Is this (the Persona) really you?"*

Obviously not.

And our search shall continue.

WHY THE PERSONA?
Here, my creative friend, we could pause and ask: *"Why does the Persona exist in the first place?"*

This mystery has puzzled many seekers of truth, for as long as humanity has existed.

According to Perennial Philosophy, the existence of the Persona—that is, humanity being equipped with an automatic, reactive "self," the Persona (and the complete unawareness of the problem) is part of a larger Game of Life.

Ancient esoteric texts present the rules of this cosmic game this way:

Humanity is born incomplete (unaware) with the feeling of

being separated from the rest of creation. It is our job, as human beings, to move into awareness in order to evolve. Our goal is to move from fragmentation to integration/oneness. Individually, this is done through a transformation.

Again, you might insist: *"But why is it so painful and complicated? Why aren't we, instead, just born fully aware, with the complete knowledge of the interconnectedness of everything?"*

This is a complex question that can only be answered through direct experience, not discourse. **The answer lies in the experience of life itself.**

However, my creative friend, what I can tell you is that your life is a gift—a process always in motion. And that the search for the self—the quest that you're on—leads to freedom. Unbounded freedom, and truth.

YOUR BODY'S GREATEST SECRET

So far, we've explored the Persona as a mental construct (Idea System). And we've compared it to a computer virus whose only goal is self-preservation.

But, as we've mentioned in our Principles 10.1 and 10.2:

10.1. "You" are a consciousness living in a Bio-Idea System (your mind-body).

10.2. Every human being is the synthesis of an Idea System (nurture, culture) and a Bio System (biology) working together as one. You are both a biological and an ideational process. One cannot exist without the other. "You" would not exist without them.

So until now, through our exploration of the Persona, we've been looking at the self strictly as an Idea System. This is an incomplete view because we're not just made out of ideas; we're also skin, bones, and everything in between.

Therefore, in order to get the full picture, we need to take a brief tour of our human biology.

And now, it's time to share with you the big discovery of these past few years. While biologists know about this, this information might be new for you.

10/90
If I were to ask you:

What percentage of the cells of your body are actually yours, versus cells from foreign organisms (microbes) that live in your body?

Can you guess?

Here's the (slightly shocking) answer: **10 percent.**

Ninety percent of the cells in your body are nonhuman.
Only 10 percent of the cells in your body are actually "yours."

This is not a misprint. Do a simple online search to learn more.

These nonhuman cells come from microbes that are creating what's called your microbiome—your biological complex living system.

With around 100 trillion microbes living inside and on your body, scientists are only beginning to realize today how important the good and bad bacteria play in your health.

Gut health, specifically, has been the ground for puzzling discoveries. Because as it turns out, the health of your gut is directly related to your brain's health and influences your thoughts and emotions. So much so, in fact, that researchers are calling the gut "the second brain."

And as you've guessed, what lives in your gut? Microbes.

From our Principle 2, we found that:

2. Your mind-body is a complex living system.

This is an actual reality. When you look at your biology, what you call "you" becomes a fuzzy concept. Because this "you" (that you think you are) is also being created by nonhuman microbes.

How important are they?

In your body, microbes prevail by an overwhelming ratio of 9 to 1: Their presence is vital.

With this kind of realization comes a new way of looking at one-self: **We were never isolated bodies operating outside of nature; instead, we are walking ecosystems. We are an ongoing relationship with nature. We are nature.**

In a recent article in the *New York Times*, the author quotes Tom Insel, who was then the director of the National Institute of Mental Health: *"It has enormous implications for the sense of self,"* he said. *"We are, at least from the standpoint of DNA, more microbial than human. That's a phenomenal insight and one that we have to take seriously when we think about human development."*

(Peter Andrey Smith, "Can the Bacteria in Your Gut Explain Your Mood?," *New York Times Magazine*, June 23, 2015)

While these discoveries are forcing us to rethink "who" we are, they are also a major breakthrough for understanding the role of microbes in our health. The use of good bacteria could become the leading practice in the future of preventive health care.

YOU ARE A BIO-IDEA SYSTEM
—ARE YOU REALLY FREE?

We have almost reached the end of Part 1. Let's take a pause in our journey with a concept to meditate on and look again at Principle 10.2:

10.2. Every human being is the synthesis of idea systems (nurture, culture) and biosystems (biology) working together as one.

You see, I completely understand that this idea is not the easiest to digest.

"Me? A Bio-Idea System!? Of course not! I'm just me!"

Let's recap. We've started with the concept of the Persona (idea system) and how it determines how we see reality and ourselves. Next, we've looked at the microbiome, the world of microbes that are the driving force (an impressive ratio of 9 to 1) behind our physiological and mental health (biosystem).

And so now we'll take a little break in our journey. And remember, I told you to pack a sense of humor because we would need it.

Well, unpack, my creative friend. Unpack. This is the moment.

Yes, I'm very aware that this information can be challenging. So please, take the time to find the humor in it. In a sense, this is the moment where we're falling from our high horse, so to speak.

Boom.

So, "you" are not what you thought you were? Cultural influences and narratives are dictating how you see the world? And microbes might be influencing your thinking?

I get it—this is weird. This sounds very much as though we're biological robots with faulty perceptions, trapped in a reality we don't understand. It's not the kindest picture.

But if you stick around, you'll see that this is also the key that will help us open the door to real freedom and empowerment.

We have decided, together, to go on a journey to discover the ultimate reality hack: Creative Dreaming. And in order to do so, we're also discovering that, to unleash this creative power, we need to evolve. This is not an easy task. The challenge is real.

We started with this exploration of "You" as a Bio-Idea System for a very simple reason. This is the foundation of our map for Creative Dreaming.

And right now, I'm also very aware that this map seems to focus more on why certain things don't work, rather than why they do.

Yes, it's true. We are right now in the middle of Plato's Cave—and the prison is airtight. It really is.

Here, because we're on our little break, I'm going to share something with you . . .

In my job as a teacher and consultant, I work with people every day. My job is a little bit like that of a gardener. I nurture students so they can grow and succeed. I also work with clients: nonprofits and for-profit organizations. Again, working with people—this time on a larger scale. Yet the principles remain the same.

In that context, I can easily predict certain outcomes. When I use Bio-Idea Systems as a conceptual map, I know what the results of the work relationship will be. It's a constant with individuals and organizations alike, because the scale is irrelevant when you look at complex living systems (more in Part 3).

But wait . . . I'm not a psychic. So how do I know?

It's really simple. When you want to create change or launch a new project, your long-term results will always be determined by how healthy your Bio-Idea System is.

Example: I can teach two students the exact same concepts and strategies. Let's imagine both students are equally motivated.

One student (A) has a healthy sense of self (Persona) and has great microbiome health.

The other student (B) is plagued by self-doubts (Persona) and has poor microbiome health.

In the short term, the difference may not be very noticeable. If both students are passionate about the work, both can do great in class.

But in the long term—years after graduation—the difference will be dramatic. Even if student B is more talented, invariably, student A will have greater positive long-term results through his/her life and career.

This seems extremely unfair (and it is), but it's also completely logical. How your Bio-Idea System works is directly related to the long-term results you're getting in your life. Your Bio-Idea System determines everything, from how you look at life, how you think, and how you interact with others to your daily habits. All these elements combined create your reality. And the limits of your reality create your destiny.

By studying Bio-Idea Systems, you can predict patterns.

In the philosophical battle between free will (you have complete freedom in your life) versus determinism (you have no freedom; everything is predetermined), it seems that determinism wins. And if we are, indeed, prisoners living in Plato's Cave, how can we ever become free?

. . .

Now, wait!

Before you (again) attempt to throw this book at the wall (stop that already!), there is good news.

First, your Bio-Idea System (that's you) is an ongoing process. This is very important. It means it's always changing.

So today, as you're reading this, if you're doing a quick assessment of your life and you're finding out that your Persona and/or your biology are creating patterns that may be limiting you, please, don't panic. Okay?

Know that every one of us, on some level, is dealing with the same issue.

So please, hold on for just a second. This is far from being the whole story. There's actually much more to the picture . . .

And we're about to reach the most important moment in our journey.

YOUR TRUE SELF
Although so far we've been painting a very dark portrait, now it's time to introduce some dazzling light.

In our Principle 10.1, we stated:

10.1. "You" are a consciousness living in a Bio-Idea System (your mind-body).

You see, my creative friend, you are not just a Bio-idea System that runs on automatic. You are much more than that.

"You" are a consciousness *living in* a Bio-Idea System.

Pierre Teilhard de Chardin expressed this very elegantly: *"We are not human beings having a spiritual experience. We are spiritual beings having a human experience."*

And at this point of the conversation, it's important for me to mention that it doesn't matter whether you consider yourself a spiritual person (or not), for you to benefit from this idea. Call it the human spirit, call it consciousness, call it soul, call it will, or call it the True Self, as I do. The name itself is not important.

Once you realize how the Bio-Idea System works, and once you start using awareness to challenge its influence, something interesting will happen: You will find your core. You will find the real "you."

This consciousness that is the true "you," living in your mind-body, has the power to create change. This is the creative self: your True Self.

Remember my previous example with the students A and B?

What I wrote is only partially accurate. Based on a quick evaluation of a Bio-Idea System and Persona, could I possibly predict an outcome? Of course.

But would I guess right, every time? Absolutely not. In fact, I've seen spectacular transformations occur that transcended any expected outcomes. Beyond the relationship between Bio-Idea System/Persona, something else is at play. There's a space within each one of us for the unexpected. And this tiny space of possibility hides something powerful. Something big.

YOUR TRUE SELF IS POWERFUL
And now, my creative friend, comes one of the most important concepts in the Creative Dreaming Method:

The True Self has sovereignty over any Bio-Idea System.

This means that—ultimately—it doesn't matter what shape your Bio-Idea System is in to begin with (it's always changing).

What matters is how expressive your True Self (consciousness) is, and the resolve you have to unfold it through your creative gesture.

What matters is the relationship between your True Self and your creative willpower.

Previously, I've borrowed the words of Philippe Starck and talked about a "mutation." Maybe a more accurate word would be "revelation."

You are here to reveal what has been there all along.

You are here to let your light shine by unfolding your True Self.

Every one of us can do it—no matter who we are or where we are. In fact, all the greatest creatives I have ever met were out-liers—odd Black Swans no one ever saw coming.

They started with very little, just a dream. On paper, they all seemed poor candidates for any kind of creative success. They were ridiculed, bullied, and challenged in every possible way.

They did not belong. They all faced incredible personal challenges involving conflicting Bio-Idea System/Persona.

See for yourself. Learn, for example, about the lives of these great women: Coco Chanel, Frida Kahlo, Maya Angelou, or Amelia Earhart—you will find the same patterns in all of them (Check out the "Little People, Big Dreams" book series, an excellent resource for kids—and grownups).

Yet all the best creatives in the world were able to transcend all expectations because they never let their Persona, or their body, dictate what they could or could not do. They defied naysayers and proved them wrong. They defied reality and altered it—and in the process, they evolved.

The goal of the Creative Dreaming Method is to integrate an authentic creative gesture into your life. This gesture is revolutionary because it reveals the conquering nature of the human spirit: the True Self unfolding into the world. And when this happens, reality reshuffles itself.

TRADE JUDGMENT FOR JOY

Here, my creative friend, at this point in our conversation, I'd like to invite you to be gentle with yourself. You see, very often, we can get frustrated with where we are in life versus where we want to be. The gap between the two creates tension.

At first, this tension can act as a motivator. But when it lingers for a long time, we're quick to blame either ourselves or the outside world.

There's this moment when we find clarity, but it's a difficult picture to accept. We suddenly realize that we've been playing it safe. Or, perhaps, that we haven't been living authentically. And it hurts. It hurts because—deep down—we also know about our True Self. We know it's there.

We know we're capable of much, much more.

The hurt is real. So I know that this conversation about the True Self can be both a blessing and a curse. You may think, *"I know about this in my gut, but why am I not living at the level of my True Self? This seems out of reach for me!"*

If this is you, let's pause. Let's take a deep breath.

This is not an empowering question—anything related to *"Why is it not working for me?"* calls for a blame-based answer, such as *"It's because you're not enough of this, or not enough of that,"* the kind of terrible suggestion that the Persona loves to make.

You see, the Creative Dreaming Method works the other way around. From the start, it's based on acceptance and lack of judgment.

Blame—no matter whether you project it outward or inward—simply doesn't work. Blame, or judgment, is a trick of the Persona. How so? Because the only result you'll get by using blame or judgment (on yourself or others) is keeping things exactly the same. And that's what the Persona wants.

In the Creative Dreaming Method, we say, *"Be gentle with yourself,"* or *"Trade judgment for joy."* This is because joy comes automatically from experiencing the process of Creative Dreaming.

And here, my creative friend, please note that I wrote that joy comes *"from experiencing the process of Creative Dreaming."* I did not write, *"Joy will come when/if you reach this or that outcome."*

Joy comes from the process itself, and it starts from day one.

Think about this . . . If you knew you were on the path of creative success, would you have joy in your life, even in the face of obstacles?

Of course you would.

And as a Creative Dreamer, this should be your focus, and a constant reminder: Your process is a gift. It makes your life vibrant, regardless wether of you're having a good day or a bad day.

When you create, you are expressing your personal freedom and your highest potential. You are echoing Life's universal creative process.

These are amazing things to feel good about, don't you think?

THE CREATIVE DREAMING METHOD IS JOY-BASED
When you follow the Creative Dreaming Method, your process is joy-based. In Part 3, we'll talk about finding a creative project that sparks joy in your life, something connected with what I call your "superpower" (something you naturally do extremely well). The reason behind it is simple. Your natural talent is an expression of your True Self. And having the incredible chance to allow it to unfold, every day, is a gift that will bring you authentic joy.

You see, one of the greatest joys in life is to awaken to what your life truly is: a fantastic adventure, right *here*, right *now*.

And when that happens, it doesn't really matter where you are in life. You become rich in joy, instantly. It's as if you recognize at the deepest level that your life is a gift, a playground where you can grow and evolve. And that each new phase of growth brings its own reward.

Let me explain . . .

You see, a long time ago, before I became "Prof. G," I worked for decades as a successful visual artist. But because I was driven by my Persona at the time, I was never really happy. And this success (which I wasn't really enjoying) kept coming and going. I could not stabilize it, because no matter how much money I made, I had a bad habit of spending it instantly. It seemed that, no matter how hard I was trying, there was always an unknown force dragging me back down (thank you, Persona). And naturally, my life was not working. I was extremely frustrated. Then I hit a rough patch. I had a series of horrible years. I completely lost focus. At one point, I was living in a gang-ridden neighborhood in Los Angeles. I was broke. I was ashamed. And then, I became really sick—bedridden—to the point where I could only work three hours per day. I was suffering from memory loss and mental decline. And the worst thing happened: People who I thought were my friends deserted me. I had hit rock bottom.

Then, right there, something clicked.
Something hard to describe . . .

It felt as if I had been touched by grace. Suddenly there was a little spark. I reached complete clarity on what was happening—I stopped lying to myself. I decided to take responsibility for everything, but responsibility without blame. And despite the fact that I was stuck in this complete state of disarray, I chose to give my life a chance by adopting the "defiant stance." I committed to bringing joy into my life by being fully engaged in my creative process, regardless of outcome: "Right *here*, right *now*."

I experienced gratitude "for what is" and let go of the anxiety and anger over "what is not." I started writing down what was bringing me happiness, the little things: "I had a nice phone call today," "I saw a beautiful sky," "I read an inspiring book." And because, perhaps for the first time, I was fully engaged with my reality, I saw that my life—no matter how bad it was at that moment—was an adventure. And I recognized that as long as I had a pulse, I could bring about change. I could write a few more lines in this adventure story.

This profound realization was an amazing experience. At first, I took little steps to bring my health back—and it worked. Then I decided to make a change in my career and find something that would fill me with meaning. Every day became an opportunity to evolve. Slowly but surely, things started to change. I changed. And I began asking myself important questions: *"Who do I want to become ten or twenty years from now? What do I need to change to become that person?"*

For the first time in my life, I started dreaming my own dream, not the idea of success that had been imposed on me by mainstream culture, advertising, or competitive relationships (i.e., the trap of "keeping up with the Joneses"). I found my dream, and I committed to it.

And this dream was inspired by the joy of being alive.

My dream was simple, really. It was about wholeness: having a happy, loving, healthy family. Being self-expressive in my work, and making a difference. Being involved in nurturing relationships. Living close to nature.

While on paper this dream was simple, making it happen required a lot of dedication (and it still does). But the sacrifices, the hard work, and the temporary setbacks are nothing compared to experiencing the joy of living your dream.

And, as I look back at that moment in my life, I can tell you how crucial that resolve to experience joy has been—and still is today . . .

Because today, I am that person I had visualized growing into and my life is the living experience of the dream I had imagined.

Letting go of blame and experiencing the joy of the present moment has its own magic. That's why the Creative Dreaming Method is joy-based.

● Exercise: What Brings You Joy?
While in the Creative Dreaming Method I conduct workshops where the live interaction is a very important part of the learning experience, in this book format you are invited to go through a series of Q&As. Simply write your answers in the book.

This is our first step in the Method. And it's a very important one. Get full clarity about what brings you joy. Next, try imagining how you could experience it through your dream/creative project.

Try it; explore joy by asking yourself these questions:

What experiences or activities bring true joy in my life? (List ten items.)

_____

_____

_____

_____

_____

_____

_____

_____

_____

_____

Which of these experiences are the most meaningful for my personal growth? (List three.)

_____

_____

_____

What are my top dreams/creative projects that I want to bring into my life?

_____

_____

_____

_____

_____

_____

_____

_____

_____

In what way could I experience meaningful joy in my creative projects? How can I connect what I love with my creative project? What would it look like?

_____

_____

_____

_____

_____

_____

_____

_____

_____

_____

Who do I want to become ten or twenty years from now?

_____

_____

_____

_____

_____

_____

What needs to change today so I can evolve into that person?

_____

_____

_____

_____

_____

_____

_____

Here, my creative friend, I'd like to suggest you play with this Q&A at least once a year. Remember, in the Creative Dreaming Method, the process (the creative exploration) is more important than a specific, fixed "ideal" (see more in Part 2). Keep it flexible, and look at this list on a yearly basis. Feel free to modify it as you evolve.

YOU ARE A DREAM

Now, my creative friend, let's recap a little bit and review what we've been discovering so far . . . and let's talk about this dream we call reality.

The title of this book is an invitation to meditate on your own life, and experiment with it. **You Are a Dream** means that—whether you're aware of it or not—you are ever re-creating your "self," and the reality that surrounds you, with every passing moment. And this self, just like a dream, is elusive.

The very elusive nature of the self—and the reason why it's so hard to get a glimpse of what "it" truly is—comes from the way it arises.

Without awareness, it is being created automatically, as the byproduct of the relationship between your Bio-Idea System and Personal Creation Story as your Persona, perpetually caught up in the ebb and flow of life.

Like a leaf dancing in the air, propelled by the wind, the unaware self is being created in reaction to everything that surrounds it: what you hear in the news, what you see in your community, what your friends are talking about, your personal history, and so on. In addition, it's also being shaped by your microbiology: what you eat, your exposure to toxins and pollutants, the state of your microbiome and gut health, how often you spend time in nature, etc.

This occurs spontaneously by simply being alive. Your experience of life is defining simultaneously both your "self" and your reality. It happens whether you like it or not. It's happening every single day. And for you, this is as "real" as it gets.

We talked before about the Eastern philosophical concept of Maya (Sanskrit for "illusion" or "magic") to describe reality. In this context, the goal of the seeker of truth is to attempt to "see beyond the veils of Maya."

This requires skills.

You need to understand that the operation is twofold: Maya is not just reality. It's "reality/self." One unit. As quantum scientists have told us numerous times, you can't separate reality from the viewer who's observing it. By observing reality, you are influencing it.

And this goes both ways. You can't separate the viewer from the reality that surrounds him/her—because the self is being created in real time by the reality that surrounds it.

You are dreaming reality without being aware of it, because that "reality" is you.
You are a dreamer, dreaming a dream.

This "reality/self" is the perfect double lock of Plato's Cave. One lock creates the other, and vice versa.

And while this lock is almost perfect, there's a way out . . .

YOU ARE SHAPING THE DREAM
In the Creative Dreaming Method, the key out of the "reality/self" lock is to simultaneously use awareness and the friction of the creative process in your own life—and to make this your personal practice.

By combining both, you create an alchemical fire that dissolves the Persona and alters reality. In this transformative process, you reveal your True Self.

This is a deep, personal transformation.

Everything is the same, but everything is different. You perceive reality as one movement where everything is interconnected. You see the interconnectedness of reality. You shed your old "self" (Persona) and experience your "reality/self" as a universal relationship with everyone and everything else.

This intimate communion with the present moment brings an incomparable sense of peace, joy, and a clear vision that brings certainty.

From this perspective, you can co-create in the present moment. You're not caught up in the dream anymore; you are shaping it.

You Are a Dream means that your reality (while "real") is elastic—it's always changing. How you interpret it and interact with it will define how you experience it. The same situation will be experienced differently according to your level of awareness.

DON'T FORGET

Here, in order to be clear, my creative friend, I really want to insist on something . . .

For the Creative Dreaming Method to work, awareness alone (or just reading this book) is not enough. It has to be used in conjunction with a specific creative gesture—a creative project in the real world—something you are going to be working on, something that will help you stretch yourself outside of your comfort zone. This process is driven by action (see Part 3).

In the Creative Dreaming Method, we are talking about creative alchemy. A transformation. And for this transformation to occur, you need fire. And this fire only comes from the friction of opposites.

The simplest way to get this positive friction into your life is to bring forth your dream (as a creative project), releasing it into reality, and having the courage to confront whatever feedback comes forward.

This is not easy, because at first the odds may seem to be against you. You have to be defiant. You have to be bold. Your creative gesture must be defiant because you're about to face great obstacles . . .

Remember, reality resists!

As a Creative Dreamer, your mission is to plow through any obstacle.

Let's see how you can do it . . .

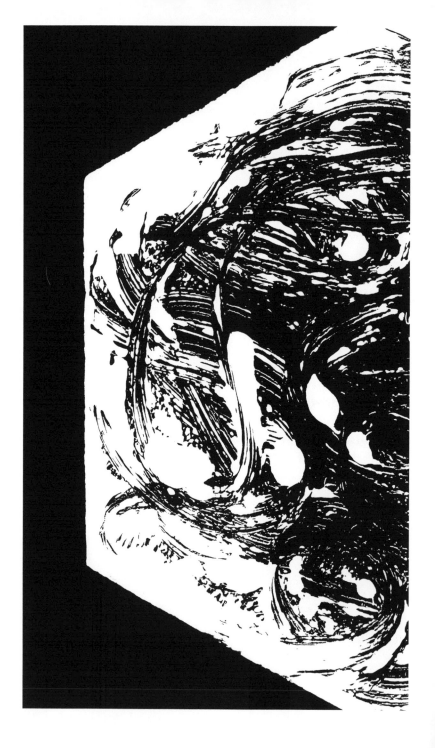

Everything in your life comes from the core.

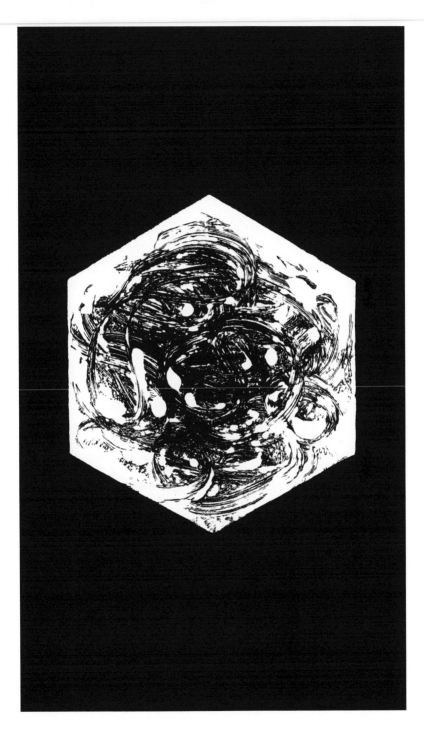

Your existence is nothing short of a miracle.
And everything in life has, in a way,
participated in it.

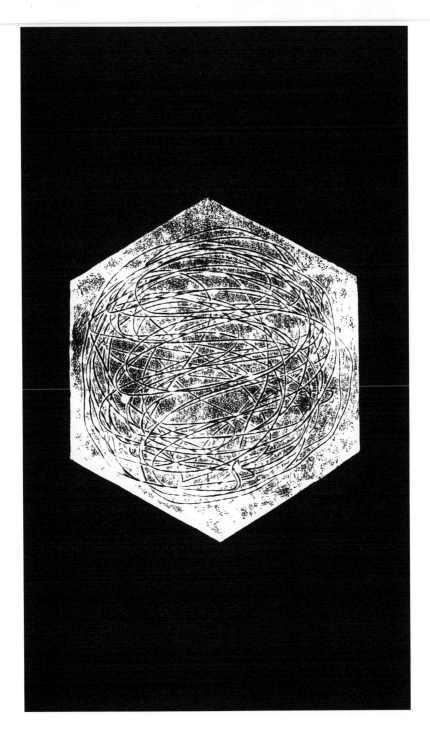

You are a relationship.

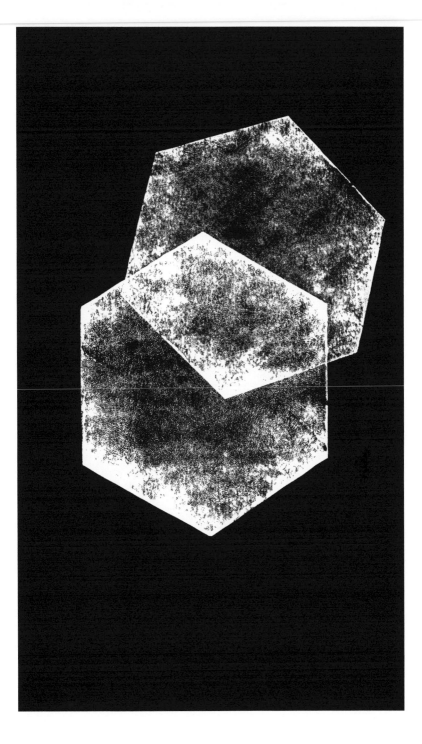

"You" are a consciousness living in a
Bio-Idea System (your mind-body).

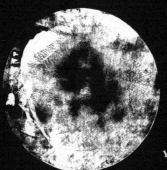

You

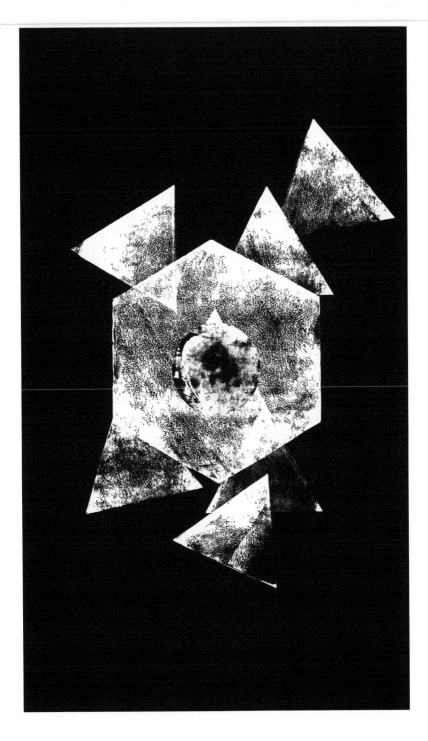

You are dreaming reality without being
aware of it, because that "reality" is you.
You are a dreamer, dreaming a dream.

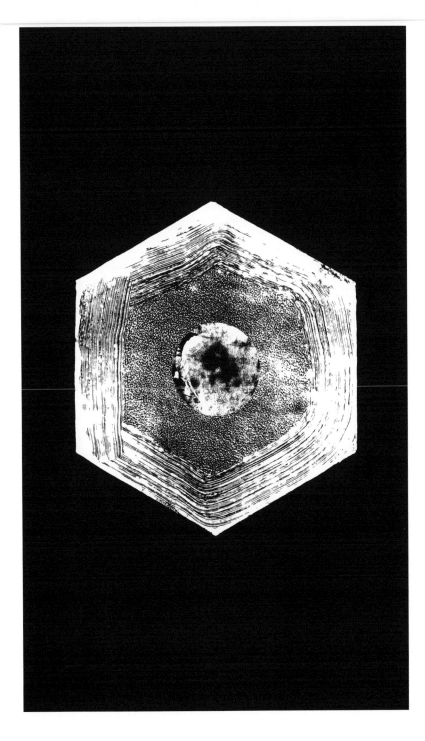

The more you practice awareness,
the more your True Self unfolds.

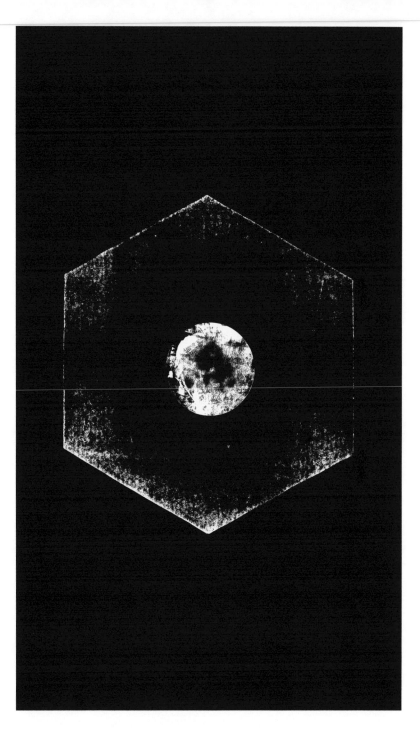

When you create, you are expressing your personal freedom and your highest potential. You are echoing Life's universal creative process.

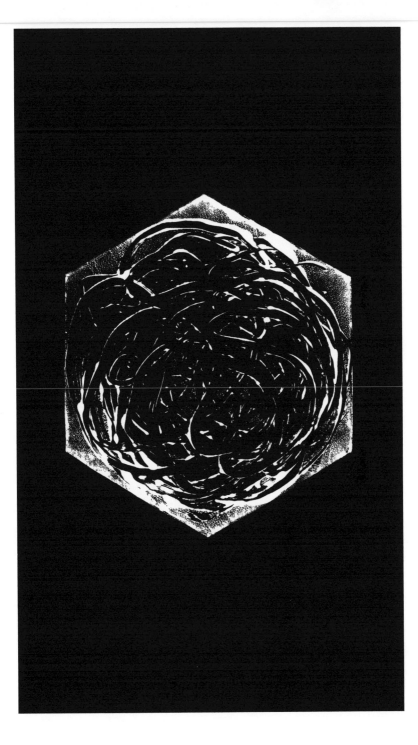

**Be bold. Dream big.
Today, what's your dream?**

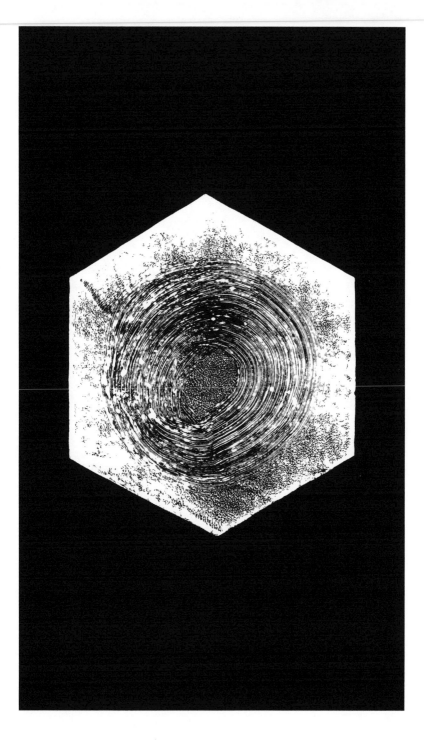

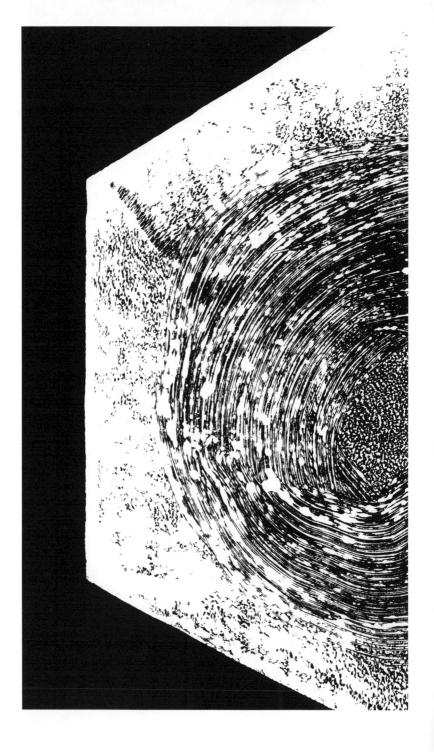

PART 2

OBSTACLES

DEALING WITH OBSTACLES

Together we've been slowly building our map for the Creative Dreaming Method. But before we continue, we now need to talk about obstacles.

Why talk about obstacles?

Because that's how professionals deal with reality.

Whether you're an artist, a creative entrepreneur, a scientist, a photographer, a healer, a writer, a painter, an artisan, a designer, a knowledge worker, a teacher, or a performer, what makes you a pro is your capacity to anticipate and deal with the obstacles of your job: You know what to do. You can handle surprises because you are prepared.

In the field of creativity, and Creative Dreaming, this skill is fundamental. **The whole process of Creative Dreaming is intimately linked with the idea of joyfully dealing with obstacles.** Without them, there's no friction and therefore, no Creative Dreaming or growth is possible.

The question is not *if* you will face obstacles in your creative journey. The question is: How will you react when you'll be faced with constant obstacles?

And here, a lot has to do with your mindset because that's what will drive the appropriate response to any event.

Obstacles are testing us to find greatness within ourselves.

As a Creative Dreamer, your mindset should be one of a champion—the champion of your own life—with one goal in mind: moving beyond any obstacle.

MASTERY AND EVOLUTION:
THE REASON FOR OBSTACLES

No matter what shape it takes, living the creative life is wonderful. It's a gift.

Think about this: Who would not want to create the life they wanted? Who would not want to be self-expressive and fully engaged in his/her life?

But living the creative life is also a privilege reserved for the few who have paid their dues.

And this is where it gets really interesting . . .

There is an initiation process that comes with creative life—any successful creative professional can attest to that. It's a "trial by fire" that will always test your skills, your patience, your intelligence, your resilience, your beliefs, and your confidence. This is why all the greatest creative visionaries in the world are also masters at handling obstacles.

Hear this: Nothing will ever go as planned!

Life will test you, every time and on every level. That's the whole point. When you bring awareness to the experience of living, you see it clearly:

The Game of Life is constantly challenging you to grow and evolve.

This is done through friction—obstacles. And this initiation process is ongoing.

Once you walk with full awareness on that path called life, you must keep growing. There's no "I've made it!" Because—no matter how great the height of your success—if you stop growing, you begin to fall.

Again, the world-class creatives all know about this. Every top creative in his/her category happens to be there because he/she pushes for ongoing creative growth. This is an ongoing process.

See our Principle 10.3:

10.3. As a Bio-Idea System, you are constantly evolving and changing. You are in relationship with —and the reflection of—Life's ongoing growth and creative process.

All you have is your process.
All you are is your process.

But it gets better. Here I'd like to share with you a curious idea about creative life by turning it around:

As a Creative Dreamer, you're building obstacles with every new idea you produce.

Your creative life is an obstacle game you're creating to achieve the satisfaction of growing, evolving, and experiencing freedom (See Part 3).

Your creative life is a game of dedication and ability. It's a relationship you've set up with Life to see how dedicated and capable you can be.

This idea can be quite challenging when you're a beginner. You might say, *"What do you mean, I've created an obstacle game? I don't want any obstacles! I just want to create. I just want to be successful and happy."*

I get it, and yet . . . I'm not sure I trust this sentence entirely. Let's hear it again: *"I don't want any obstacles! I just want to create. I just want to be successful and happy."*

Could this be a Persona statement? Think about this. *"I just want to . . ."* sounds like something easy and reasonable (a given), and then you add: *"be successful and happy,"* which are the two ultimate prizes all humanity is running after . . .

Yes, you can be successful and happy. But you need to let go of the disempowered *"I just want to"* and switch to a more radical approach, one that involves your full engagement—the defiant stance.

Such as:

"I have the complete resolve and focus to be successful and happy through my creative process. I'm willing to grow from it, and I'm willing to handle any obstacles that will come my way."

And now, if you're reading this and think, *"This is so corny!"* please tell your Persona that I recognize its cynicism, and sense of irony (touché!).

What I just wrote is not an affirmation that needs to be posted on a mirror and repeated twice a day. It's really not.

What I wrote is a state of mind that needs to be lived and experienced daily through action.

Big difference.

Successful and happy creative people have an incredible resolve to be that way. When they are confronted with obstacles (which is a lot), they become entirely focused on removing them. This is not an extra burden; it's part of their process. And here's an important insight: This process brings them joy and satisfaction.

I think this is extremely important to get—as I've stated before:

You have to be defiant with Life. Joyfully defiant.

You need to connect with the inner fire at the center of your being. The fire that's unstoppable. And this energy can express itself in numerous ways.

You can be gentle and unstoppable—I've seen it in a wonderful woman with whom I had the pleasure to work with when I was young. She was the founder of a very influential store in Paris. She was an unstoppable gentle power. A calm strength. And I've seen her triumph over incredible obstacles using this energy. This was amazing to watch.

The defiance I'm talking about is nothing like bravado. It's a silent, centered power that comes from your True Self—your inner core. One that says: *"I have full presence in this task."*

And once you reconnect with this power in your own life (because we all have it), everything changes.

The drive to dream and create is an energy that comes from your True Self expressing itself into the world. Your True Self moving into awareness through your creative gesture.

This process of becoming is directly connected with the process of mastery.

The more you're able to master your practice, the more your True Self unfolds into life.

Mastery is the gift that comes from the fully engaged creative life; and true mastery comes from years of sustained effort. It's the byproduct of consistent, intelligent hard work. When you reach that level, what seems complicated for others is effortless for you because you're used to blasting through obstacles.

Mastery is the unfolding of your True Self through your creative expression.

In complete opposition, the part that says, *"I don't want any obstacles!"* is the Persona that doesn't want any change to occur—status quo thinking. And status quo thinking is the enemy of creativity because it's about keeping things (and people) the way they are.

You see, my creative friend, **the movement of your True Self is set toward awareness, creativity, discovery, aliveness, character, and determination.**

In contrast, the movement of your Persona is set in the oppo-site direction. It's set toward unawareness, comfort, gratifica-tion, conformity, entitlement, laziness, and apathy.

Please note that you can't move in two opposite directions simultaneously. You have to be very clear on this with your-self—and know where you're going.

Through its numerous obstacles, the authentic creative life reveals your True Self, and in the process, dissolves the Persona. Creative life and Creative Dreaming is a process of profound transformation. That's the real secret. But it's a pro-cess to be experienced—reading about it is not enough.

And, obviously, for this "alchemical" process to occur, you need friction. You need obstacles. Every obstacle you face is a test that challenges you to improve. And the more you grow creatively, the more you're able to tackle greater obstacles. Creative growth feeds upon itself.

THE GOLD OF THE ALCHEMISTS
In Creative Dreaming, your intent should be focused and radically minded. In our conversation together, I keep reinforcing, *"You have to be defiant with Life."* This is key.

You've probably heard this Latin expression before: **magnum opus**, or "the great work." It's often used in a creative context to describe the most important work of an artist.

This expression has its origins in the ancient art of alchemy. Alchemists were seekers of truth, dedicated to what they called the Great Work: the evolution of mankind. The "gold" of the alchemists was to produce a transformed, unified individual, reconnected with the Whole. But today's use of the expression "magnum opus" is out of context. It's incomplete . . . something is missing.

In the original Latin, the old manuscripts spoke of **magnum opus contra naturam** or "great work against nature."

This contra naturam, or "against nature," is the friction we've been talking about together. Creative Dreaming needs this friction—because in order to bestow its gift, reality demands it.

Here I'd like to ask you to imagine for a moment nature/life/reality as being a teacher.

An epic teacher: transpersonal, supra-conscious, cross-dimensional—unbounded and unlimited. A teacher beyond time and space. In our story, you decide one day to knock on the teacher's door to get the ultimate reward: freedom, and the discovery of your True Self.

> You knock twice.
>
> You hear footsteps.
>
> Slowly, the teacher opens the door.
>
> *"I'd like to become a Creative Dreamer,"* you say.
>
> The teacher looks deep into your eyes, and . . .

And now let's pause the story. Let's suppose that the teacher is interested in supporting your request . . . Let me ask you this: In our story, what do you think will happen?

Will the teacher give you the gift right away, and promptly close the door?

or,

Will the teacher invite you to become his student and for years test you repeatedly through numerous trials so you can transform into the person worthy of receiving the gift?

Think about it.

You already know the answer, don't you?

All good stories talk about growing through ongoing effort. Authentic transformation is never easily acquired. And there's a reason why . . .

The gift is more than the actual outcome—or the realization of your initial dream: It's the process of transformation taking place while you're on the path.

The gift of your creative life is the process itself.

You see, my creative friend, you and I are so small in comparison with the mighty teacher that is nature/life/reality. Our defiance—our desire to create the new—is the call of our True Self. This is the most authentic part of our humanity. The part that thirsts for oneness.

Our defiance, the friction of reality (obstacles), the desire to create the new—these are all part of one larger Whole.

See it. Honor it.

In the Creative Dreaming Method, our goal is to refine our process by bringing awareness into every aspect of our lives. This focused awareness reveals the beauty of the Whole.

LET'S GET STRATEGIC

I hope that, through this introduction, I was able to reframe how you see the obstacles in your life. Please know that every challenge you will encounter hides a breakthrough. Looking at every challenge as a meaningful opportunity to grow is a mindset that allows you to see—and interact with—reality in an empowered way.

Here, we're going to take a brief tour of the most common obstacles you will face in your creative journey. Some are internal; some are external.

Please note that these obstacles are always interconnected—they exist in relationship with the Whole, which always includes external reality and your internal perception of it. For example, an obstacle that seems to be strictly external (such as a world event that might block your project) is also simultaneously internal (your perception of the event and how you decide to interpret and deal with it).

As we go through these obstacles, you'll see that we're going to explore the many tricks of the Persona. As always, please bring your sense of humor while we uncover them.

Here, I'm listing these obstacles in a sequential order to simplify reading, but know that, when they appear, they can show up in bundles.

OBSTACLE 1: LACK OF AWARENESS

Lack of awareness, or "going unaware" while being awake, is the number-one obstacle to Creative Dreaming. It's the tool your Persona will use every time in order to attempt to make you fail with your creative project.

Unawareness can take millions of forms, and if you're wondering, *"Why don't we live in a happier world where everyone could easily create the life they wanted? Why so much struggle?"* unawareness is always a big part of the answer.

To understand how unawareness can creep into our lives, let's quickly look at nature first. Go into any natural environment—say, a forest—and observe attentively.

You will see struggle everywhere you look: Trees compete for access to light and nutrients. Plants fight for space. Animals eat each other. Bacteria are in a constant state of warfare. It's survival of the fittest, all the way.

Yet—watch out! This is just a very superficial way to look at things. We need to go deeper, because there's more to the picture . . . There's something at work that we can't see—a hidden structure that only unfolds when we enlarge our perspective of time.

If you observe nature long enough (for decades), you will discover patterns. You'll find out that every animal species depends on one another, and together they form a unified symbiosis. This is true even in the relationship between predators and prey—they depend on each other to survive. If either prey or predator outnumbers the delicate balance at work, a global collapse ensues.

The struggle you see in nature is always part of a greater whole: a complex, unified, living system unfolding. And the popular notion of "survival of the fittest" is actually very misleading. On a larger scale, it's always "survival through interdependence." Every biologist will confirm this fact—it's a universal law of nature.

Unfortunately, we (the silly humans) still culturally operate under the "survival of the fittest" notion, even if it's clear that this approach is leading us to certain oblivion. Most of humanity doesn't understand (or care) that our survival can only happen through a mutual interdependence with nature (Principles 3, 4, and 5).

Not understanding our interdependence with our environment is the greatest expression of unawareness manifesting itself throughout humanity. We know that we're interconnected. Scientists have told us for decades how interdependent with nature we truly are. Yet we still don't get it.

But why is it so?

Let's take a simple example. Now imagine you're at the beach. You see a middle-aged man sitting on the sand. He's looking at the horizon, a can of soda in hand. He finishes his drink, crushes the can, and places it next to him. After fifteen minutes or so, he stretches a bit, stands up, and walks back to his car, leaving the can behind him—while a trash can stands just twenty feet away!

If you've seen something like that and politely inquire about "what's really going on" (as I sometimes do), the polluter will simply say, *"Oh! I did not see the trash can."* Or, *"I just forgot."*

Is it an easy cop-out? Or is there something else here at play?

First, let's state the obvious: When you know that a soda can contains 39 grams of sugar (yes, that's about ten sugar cubes); it's easy to understand that this incredible amount will create havoc in the brain. In fact, research shows that high levels of sugar hinder learning and memory by slowing down the brain, contribute to depression and anxiety, and are a risk factor for cognitive decline and dementia. Yes . . . all this in a soda can! In other words, if you're interested in your own health, and if dementia doesn't seem an engaging prospect for your future, stay away from sodas.

But let's go back to our polluter . . .

While it's easy to blame an individual (who is on a toxic sugar high), it's much more valuable to understand the larger picture. And here it becomes really interesting.

Everything you see that's not life affirming in an individual (such as trashing the environment) is always connected to unawareness. This curious moment when an individual "goes unconscious" while being awake.

Conversely, the capacity for understanding interdependence starts with a sense of self-awareness.

The polluter does not trash the beach because he actively wants to destroy nature (I sincerely hope that, in the morning, he doesn't jump out of bed saying, *"Today, I'm destroying the planet!"*). He pollutes because he's forgetful, or simply doesn't care. He's living in a strange interzone, disconnected and unconscious, while being fully awake. He's a functional sleepwalker, meaning that he's incapable of understanding connections that go beyond his immediate proximity or his personal comfort.

Even if the polluter thinks he's fully aware, perhaps saying to himself, *"It doesn't make a difference, the beach is full of trash, anyway,"* or, *"Someone else will pick this up."* The faulty logic, and lack of understanding of the big picture reveals the state of unawareness. And, unfortunately, our beach polluter is not alone: Most of humanity is deeply asleep as they go through life.

Again, why?

As we saw earlier, Life unfolds as a creative process—regardless of whether we decide to participate in it or *not*. This creative process is completely neutral. If you bring awareness and participate in it, this force can inspire you to be the best you can be and **your life can become a wonderful dance of creation.** If you don't, the very same force will lead you astray.

Remember, when you bring awareness to your creative process, you are co-creating it. When you're unaware of its presence, it will run you like a machine (through your Persona).

Life's creative process is the most powerful force you can imagine. Yet, when you deny its existence or are simply unaware of it, it has the power to destroy you and everything around you. This is the dark side of this natural force—because the creative process is both light and darkness, and it expresses itself in our reality in infinite ways, shapes, and forms. Because we have indeed, as humans, the capacity to inquire, reflect, imagine, and make decisions, we are uniquely built for awareness and creative thinking. And according to our current understanding of the natural world, it appears that we're the only creatures doing so (although science is starting to recognize that many life forms are much more intelligent and aware than we previously thought).

Awareness and creative thinking are the gift we've received from Life. We all have it. This gift is extremely important—it's humanity's treasure.

But this gift comes with a set of responsibilities. First, we need to use it, and to stop pretending it's not there. Next, we need to use it intelligently, and with integrity, by being of service to the Whole.

If, instead, we go unaware, and out of laziness, greed, or sheer stupidity, act as if we were disconnected from everything else, Life's creative process shows its destructive aspect—creative darkness kicks in. It works as a self-regulating mechanism. It can operate on a large scale or on an individual level, but most likely on both, simultaneously. And when that happens, it's brutal.

WHY UNAWARENESS APPEARS IN YOUR LIFE
Being asleep while living—or being in a permanent state of unawareness—is the lot of humanity. Because we are Bio-Idea Systems, there are both biological and ideational reasons for it.

Biologically, our brain has the habit of going unaware quite a lot—possibly to save energy. Even while fully awake, our brain self-regulates to slower frequencies throughout the day, depending on the situation. A classic example is the phenomenon of "highway hypnosis." After you've been driving for a few hours, your brain switches to "auto-mode" which allows you to relax while still being able to control the vehicle (this is actually very dangerous). The same thing happens while learning at school, attending a lecture, or listening to a business presentation: The brain naturally slows down to a state of receptive relaxation. In that state, your brain focuses on one task only, and you become less aware of your surroundings.

The list is almost infinite: driving, learning, attending a public presentation, shopping, relaxing, viewing a film in a theater, watching TV, taking a shower or a bath, cooking, drawing, listening to music, playing, jogging, eating, making love—almost every moment in our lives is an opportunity for the brain to slow down and go unaware.

If you think about it for a moment, this notion is quite shocking. Another way to look at this would be to ask, *"What are the actual moments when we are we not sleepwalking?"*

But that's not all . . .

In addition, we are culturally conditioned to limit our thinking time and to instead "listen to the experts." It starts with our family unit and our school, and it continues with our religious education and, later, our workplace—it's understood that "deep thinking" is not needed in the context of social life. It's actually frowned upon. The reason invoked for this conditioning is based on keeping things practical. The rationalization being: *"You can't overthink everything."*

Structurally, every society, organization, or group (a complex living system) benefits in its efficacy from having every part of its system working in unison. If one part (an individual) pauses and starts to question everything, the whole organization cannot operate the same way—it has to either reject the dissonant voice or reorganize itself and evolve. The former is easier.

As you can see, there are biological, cultural, and practical reasons for unawareness. But at the individual level, unawareness also comes from the Persona—it is its favorite tool.

Your Persona uses unawareness on you in order to maintain its existence. Unawareness is actually the most potent tool available to the Persona, and it uses it at every opportunity.

By making you unaware and encouraging you to be a functioning sleepwalker, your Persona takes over your life and it gets to survive.

HOW TO BE MORE AWARE
In Part 1, we've already explored a practice to raise awareness (see "**Daily Practice: Is This Really Me?**" on page 95).

Here, I'd like to expand on this idea a bit more.

In order to gain a greater sense of awareness, the prime strategy of the Creative Dreaming Method is to use your creative project as a tool for exploration and transformation (see Part 3). A deepening of awareness is one of the gifts of the creative life.

If you think about it, a person who has no creative practice—a consumer—has very few daily opportunities to experience awareness (shopping is closely related to sleepwalking). However, when you create something (a business, an art practice, a meaningful relationship, or an authentic experience), you are automatically setting up a feedback loop mechanism with reality that will tell you how well you're doing. You're entering into a fully aware, active relationship with Life. Once you have this awareness, your life becomes a ground for exploration, discovery, and growth.

In that sense, the creative act forces you to practice awareness by confronting the Persona. Each new creative experiment makes you evolve.

This is not easy. But if you're able to pass beyond the Persona's resistance to change, you will discover that your life is, and has always been, a creative practice.

PRACTICE: THE PERSONA AWARENESS JOURNAL

The Persona Awareness Journal (PAJ) is an uncommon journaling practice that is meant to be used alongside a creative project. Note that it should always be attached to a specific project. That is, never use it alone.

The goal of the Persona Awareness Journal is to outwit the Persona by writing everything negative it says and looking at it with full awareness—with three questions for every entry.

It's really simple.

Here's how it works. While you work on your creative project, every time you catch a fear, or a movement toward unawareness (like spending hours on social media instead of working), you simply write down what the obstacle is (by describing what's happening), then you answer these three questions:

1. Is this a valid point, or is it the Persona at work?

2. If this is the Persona, what is it gaining from it?

3. How can I move beyond this?

Notes on question 1.
Is this a valid point, or is it the Persona at work?
If, in fact, "this is a valid point," then your job is to define a plan of action to take care of the problem. A lot of times, you'll find a real problem (example: running out of cash on a project); and, along with it, you'll find an interpretation of what that means (example: *"I can't ever get organized with money"*). Watch out—make sure you become an expert at separating the facts from these interpretations. These interpretations are the reflection of your Persona at work.

Notes on question 2.
If this is the Persona, what is it gaining from it?
The answer to this question is almost always the same: The Persona wants things and situations to stay the same. The Persona does not want you to change, so it can continue to exist the way it is. The Persona is always against creative projects (because they encourage change and growth).

Notes on question 3.
How can I move beyond this?
The secret to moving beyond any obstacle is twofold. First, you can take care of it directly by setting up a plan and acting on it. Second, you need to figure out how you can evolve internally so this obstacle never comes back into your life. This is the opportunity for growth. Another way to ask yourself this question is: *"How can I change/grow to move beyond this?"*

PERSONA AWARENESS JOURNAL: EXAMPLE

Here's a real-life example on how to use the Persona Awareness Journal.

But before we go into it, there's a twist!

I'll share the story in an interesting way—by presenting you with two alternative endings.

First, I'm going to share with you what could have happened—but did not (the predictable pattern).

And next, I'll share with you what actually happened (the creative success). Please note: I've changed the name and some details in the story to respect the privacy of the individual mentioned.

MEET LAURA

Meet our friend Laura, a thirtysomething mom of two, who, one beautiful spring day, decides to write and self-publish her first book.

As with any creative endeavor, there's anxiety linked with the project. After all, she has never done it before. She's thinking (or her Persona is thinking): *"Will it work? Am I good enough?"*

The process goes like this: Laura gets to work on her project and ends up spending ten grueling months writing her manuscript. Later, she hires a copy editor and a graphic designer. During this time, she keeps second-guessing herself. Her Persona impersonates her and says, *"Am I good enough to do this?"* She cringes every time she works. But she keeps at it, even when it's hard. Many times she catches herself wasting time on social media instead of actually writing (unawareness alert!). But after more than a year of effort, she finally prints her book. It's now available online—all is well. She did it!

And, guess what? Nothing happens.

Beyond her friends and family, she doesn't sell any copies. She gets really frustrated. Her Persona is quick to cry the disempowering *"No one cares!"* Yet Laura dries her tears and hires a promotional "expert" to get her book featured on a few blogs. And after thousands of dollars spent on several blog tours and one small article in a magazine, still, nothing.

All of a sudden, a horrible feeling creeps in: the strange horror that only comes with the taste of creative failure. Her Persona rushes in to make Laura go unaware even more. She hears in her head: *"I knew it! I'm not good enough. I've made a terrible mistake! All of this time and money for nothing!"* She feels horrible; she's depressed.

The Persona wins.

Laura joins the list of the millions of frustrated creatives who were never rewarded for their talents. Years later, she's bitter. Every time she hears about "creativity," she feel a knot in her stomach.

The End (of what did not happen).

Okay, now . . . Here's what really happened. Laura is a dear (and talented) friend who actually learned about the Persona through our many conversations. Years ago, she had initially approached me to talk about self-publishing, but our discussions always ended up going to the Persona—and defining strategies to go beyond it. So when she started her book project, she had a solid plan. She was ready.

From the start, Laura knew that—like all creatives—she had her self-doubts. She knew the games her Persona loved to play on her. One evening, after a long, long talk with her partner, she decided to start her Persona Awareness Journal, and to use it every time she started second-guessing herself or went unaware instead of working (through procrastination: mindless social media browsing, napping, daydreaming, etc.).

As she began her project, she filled up the journal with her Persona's self-created worries. Every time she caught her Persona acting out, she wrote it down in the journal. And, slowly, it became a game. In the evenings, she started sharing her best/worst Persona moments of the day from her journal. *"These conversations were some of the most illuminating I've ever had,"* she told me later on.

And the game became funnier every day because she started seeing the humor of the situation. The journal filled up with nonsensical fears and distractions. The more she was working, the more she saw her Persona at work. She plowed through all the resistance, and by the end of the book, she looked at her journal and saw how silly everything was.

Now that the book was completed, she felt stronger and more confident. She felt a change inside.

Laura published her book and—just like in our previous story— nothing happened. At first, she was devastated—all her greatest fears grabbed her. Again, she wrote it all in the journal. And again, she discovered how her Persona was working against her.

Yet, through this feedback process, Laura realized she was missing something. To be successful in self-publishing, she needed to learn about one vital skill: self-promotion. She hated the idea (or her Persona did), but she took a stab at it. One day at a time, she connected with blogs, and once again, nothing happened. Then, one day, one blog said "yes." She got a write-up. Realizing how difficult the process was, she decided to write about it in her own blog . . . She documented every step, every hurdle she experienced. The blog grew and attracted readers—creatives who could relate with her situation. Slowly, she began building a fan base. And naturally, her fan base started buying her book.

After five years of constant work—and many, many changes, Laura is now both creatively and financially successful. More important, she's a different person altogether. *"Looking at the old journal today,"* she told me, *"it's crazy to see how scared I was about almost everything. It's hilarious to see this now because I've changed so much."*

The End.

Make sure you experiment with the Persona Awareness Journal; it's a fantastic tool to help you get through the obstacles/phases of growth you will experience through your creative journey. The more you use awareness in conjunction with your creative project, the easier things will get.

WHY THE PERSONA AWARENESS JOURNAL WORKS

The simple process of the Persona Awareness Journal is actually inspired by cybernetics and design thinking. Let's go back to our previous metaphor that compared the Persona to a computer virus.

If the Persona acts like a computer virus, equipped with a perfect loop mechanism with one function (keeping the status quo by preventing creativity), then the only way out is to create a counter-loop with the opposite effect (dissolving the status quo, encouraging creativity).

The reason why the Persona Awareness Journal is so effective is that we rarely get to see our own thoughts and biases on paper. When we do so, we start recognizing the mechanical patterns of the Persona. And here, of course, it's important (again) to have a sense of humor—and take what we uncover with a grain of salt. Acceptance and lack of judgment are key.

Remember, it's not so much the actual content (what the Persona says or does) that's important, it's the fact that you're recognizing a pattern. When you see the pattern clearly, it's easy to move beyond it by going back to your creative work.

The counter-loop you create works as follows:

> **1.** You are working on your creative project and your journal is ready (you bring awareness to your process).
> **2.** The Persona panics (*"Change is coming!"*).
> **3.** The Persona will try to plunge you into unaware-ness to prevent you from succeeding with your task (through emotions, self-doubts, status quo thinking,

over-the-top interpretations of what certain events mean, rationalizations, generalizations, or distractions).

4. When you notice one of the Persona's attempts, simply put it in writing in the journal. No matter how weird-sounding it may be, you don't judge what you uncover (or yourself). You just get back to work.

5. You acknowledge and celebrate your victory over the Persona's shenanigans. You're growing and innovating through your work. Go back to Step 1.

The Persona Awareness Journal works because the more your Persona is acting out, the more you have material to put in your journal. The more material you uncover, the easier it is to see the trappings of the Persona and move beyond it.

This method is similar to using feedback mechanism in design thinking (more in Part 3). By launching the project into the real world, the ongoing feedback you get (here, from the Persona) drives the process of discovery. As long as you stick with it, you'll benefit from growth (regardless of outcome).

Introducing the Persona into your creative process, and treating it playfully (as in Laura's example), is a really efficient counter-loop to the Persona's self-sabotage attempts. The more you get to know it, the easier you can get beyond it.

GO-GETTERS BEWARE: UNAWARENESS PROJECTED OUTWARD

What we just discovered is unawareness projected inward (through self-doubts, fears, etc.), which is very common with creative people who are introverts.

However, if you're an extrovert, you might not have

any of these challenges to deal with because you are focused solely on action and getting things done.

But displacing a lack of focus by projecting unawareness outward through action is another trick of the Persona. It can be equally destructive.

A classic mistake extroverts make is to start a creative project without taking the time to properly understand the culture of their audience, or the spirit of the times (see Part 3).

For example, I've seen it with highly successful "go-getters" (aka Type A personalities) who thought they were convincing everyone around them to support their projects—without actually listening to feedback.

What was happening was that they were so gung-ho about moving forward with their ideas that they were presenting them in a way that was extremely matter-of-fact (domineering), leaving no space to challenge them or to explore alternatives. In doing so, they were receiving no real feedback and were refusing to acknowledge reality. All that mattered to them was "to be right" (a classic Persona move).

Every time, the pattern was the same: These individuals had had incredible successes in the past, and they used these past references as a way to prove to themselves (and to the world) that their new projects were foolproof.

Their critical mistake was failing to understand that the world had changed. By refusing to learn about the present moment, understand their audience, and connect with the spirit of the times—and therefore staying in their comfort zone—they created projects that failed.

Here, the Persona says: *"Let's act and simply keep doing what we know—we'll be fine."* If you listen to it, you will act based on the past ("what we know"). This is where the trap hides. In the short term, it can work, but in the long term, it's always devastating. "Living on past successes" equals "living in the past."

Not good.

This pattern is not limited to individuals. It can also happen in very large companies and can result in spectacular failures.

If you are one of these "go-getters," the solution is to slow down. Be smart by surrounding yourself with advisers (known for their vision and for their understanding of the times) whose job is to give honest feedback and ask tough questions. Obstacles and resistance can be an important part of your success, if you acknowledge them and handle them in a way that will allow you to explore the new.

If you do so, you'll still be able to move mountains through action, but you'll do it in the right direction (see Part 3).

. . .

We're going to continue looking at some other obstacles you might encounter. Please note that the structure is always the same, inward or outward: These obstacles are tools connected to the Persona to make you "go unaware." The solution is always the practice of awareness and the feedback from the creative process itself.

OBSTACLE 2: FEAR AND STATUS QUO THINKING

Another way the Persona can make you go unaware is by using the emotion of fear to paralyze you. Because fear has the power to bypass critical thinking, it's a perfect ally for the Persona. Sometimes, fear is something that's been passed on through generations—or peers—by what's called status quo thinking. This fear-based mode of thinking supports inaction as a way to "keep everything safe." We see it through expressions such as: *"We never make any waves"* or *"The tall poppy gets cut down,"* or horror stories such as *"Your grandpa lost all his fortune because he also tried to . . ."*

Fear often comes from fantastical ideas connected with past or future events. It thrives on inaction.

Two classic creative fears are:

> **The fear of failure:** If I fail, people are going to mock me. If I fail, my life will be over—disaster will strike.

> **The fear of success:** If I succeed, I'll have more problems. I'll lose the joy in my life because of jealousy from others. I'll get overwhelmed by the burden of responsibility that comes with success.

Please note that these fears (failure or success) are fears about change. The Persona doesn't want anything to change—keeping things the way they are is its number one priority.

Fears generated by the Persona are always overdramatic—like a bad soap opera. In real life, you can either fail or succeed— this is just feedback at one point in time. If you've set up your

Creative Dreaming practice correctly, none of these temporary outcomes should create any problem in the long term because they are part of your process (see Part 3). Your long-term process is what counts.

Fears (like the Persona) only see things in black or white. This is not how the world works. Fears of success or failure both create a loopy mind trap by trying to guess what the future will be like, which is impossible.

You can get rid of these fears by practicing awareness and focusing on the present moment (see Persona Awareness Journal) as you're focusing on the task at hand.

As a reminder, say to yourself: *"Back to the present!"*

Once you act and get actual results, you'll see that those fears were unfounded to begin with.

OBSTACLE 3.1: THE DESIRE FOR PERFECTION

The desire for perfection is a common obstacle for all creatives. And it expresses itself in infinite variations. The first thing you need to know is that "perfection" is just a mental construct that's disconnected from actual reality. You can't ever reach it. And because you can't reach it, it prevents you from engaging meaningfully with your reality.

To illustrate this, we're going to take a look at an all-time favorite. I've heard this sentence countless times coming from creatives:

"I'm still trying to figure out what I truly want exactly. It has to be perfect."

Waiting for "perfection" creates an unattainable image, an image so distant from actual reality that it always leads to inaction or what I call "paralysis from analysis." Get this: Perfection doesn't exist. Period.

Formulating the "perfect" plan is a trap that presupposes the existence of an ideal life (*"what I truly want"*)—without realizing that this "ideal" is a complete fantasy created by the Persona, with no relationship to reality (what is).

Every fantasy (the perfect project, the perfect moment, the perfect partner, the perfect plan, the perfect life, etc.) is dangerous because it's a fixed image that doesn't evolve and is completely disconnected from real life. The reason this approach leads to paralysis is that, once this "ideal image" is found (if ever), there's a fear that you'll never be good enough to realize it. Hence, to avoid being disappointed, the Persona convinces you that it's better not to act on it and to keep "figuring out" the perfect plan. The desire for perfection is, indeed, a "perfect trap" that leads to frustration and inaction. It's the opposite of the true creative process.

Again, forget about perfection—it doesn't exist! Instead, launch your project on a small scale, and simply call it "an experiment." Be curious and see what happens. That way, you're removing the pressure of a possible "failure" because you're just getting feedback from the real world (good or bad) through your experiment. In doing so, you'll gain a real insight on *"what you truly want,"* and you'll build valuable experience that will keep you moving forward.

"What you truly want" is never an outcome that you can imagine or control in advance. ***"What you truly want"* is the**

knowledge that arises in the present by interacting with reality. The experience of life hides the gem.

Remember our Principle 10.3:

10.3. As a Bio-Idea System, you are constantly evolving and changing. You are in relationship with—and the reflection of—Life's ongoing growth and creative process.

All you have is your process.
All you are is your process.

The more you live, and experience life (try, fail, try again, succeed), the more you'll know what you want. You and life are an ongoing living process, not a perfect ideal.

OBSTACLE 3.2: SEEKING THE APPROVAL OF OTHERS

This obstacle is closely related to the desire for perfection—here, it's being projected outward onto the "others." Whatever this actually means . . . You could start by asking yourself: *"Who are these imaginary others, really?"* and *"By what mysterious authority can they give me approval on what I'm doing today?"*

Don't be fooled. This is another sly trick from the Persona. By saying, *"I should get the approval of others,"* what's implied is that you can only create if you don't make any waves. Therefore you must: avoid conflict, stay away from ridicule, be accepted by all, etc. And sadly, this also implies that if you need approval, it means that you're not good enough to begin with. That you are not "perfect."

This—excuse my French—is highly messed up. Know that if you're good enough to read this book and be curious about your creativity, then you're good to go to live your life on your own terms. You don't need validation from anyone.

So watch out, because if you fall for it, the Persona will entrap you in a game you will never win.

Why?

Because, when it comes to creativity (or simply, life), you can't ever "get the approval of others." It simply doesn't exist! There will always be someone, somewhere, who will not like what you do. And that's completely fine. Get comfortable with this.

Because your creative gesture is always in opposition to the status quo, things are going to change. You will make waves; some people will get jealous; others will try to stop you in weird, passive-aggressive ways. That's how it works.

And at the end of the day, it's no big deal. Creative life is a bumpy ride.

If a so-called "friend" doesn't approve of your creative project, it has nothing to do with you, but entirely with him/her. When you create, you become like a mirror—everyone around you is forced to ask, *"Why am I not doing that, too?"* And—thanks to the Persona—it's now easier for your frustrated friend to "be right" by joining the ranks of the proverbial "haters' club," rather than being inspired by your dedication and giving you encouragement. You see, this has nothing to do with you and it should not be your concern.

At the end of the day, it boils down to one thing:

Haters hate because they don't create.

This is very common. And if some old friends try to sabotage your creative energy, it's time for an upgrade; you deserve better. Go out there and make new friends. That's why real creatives tend to hang out together—we support each other.

Life is not a game of validation; it's more like resistance training. The resistance that Life places in front of you has a very important purpose: It builds your willpower. It strengthens your character.

Follow your creative process and every day, you'll achieve little wins. That's how you'll get authentic, healthy, inner validation. That's where the real gold is.

OBSTACLE 4: BEING A DILETTANTE

A dilettante (or a dabbler) is someone who cultivates a momentary interest in a field, such as a subgenre of the arts, without ever being committed to it. The dilettante has the habit of getting into an activity and then switching to a different one every few months or so. You can find numerous versions of the dilettante in every aspect of life: the dilettante entrepreneur, the dilettante artist, the dilettante boyfriend/girlfriend, the health dilettante, etc.

The "dilettante syndrome" is probably one of the greatest tricks the Persona can play on someone because the dilettante is being led to think that he's living the authentic creative life (after all, he's working on so many creative projects). But in fact, he's not. The dilettante is not a real creative because he avoids all of the meaningful growth that should come with the creative process. In that sense, he's afraid to commit because he's afraid to evolve. Fear of change is what controls the dilettante.

By changing his interests on a continual basis, the dilettante always stays the same (and that's what the Persona wants). The dilettante is stuck in a creative arrested development; often, he's stuck in his life as well.

Many dilettantes are very capable (and intelligent). And because of their innate talent, they somehow believe they can avoid (or outsmart) the responsibilities of the creative process without any consequences. But in doing so, they're also avoiding its true rewards.

Being a dilettante is a tough obstacle to go around. In a sense, it can be compared to addiction because the dilettante is in denial that there's a problem—*"Look,"* he says, *"I've been doing so many things!"*

The way through this dead end is to bring full awareness to the actual creative results (or lack thereof) the dilettante is producing by asking tough questions:

What are the results you've actually produced by being a dilettante? Are these results really matching what you're capable of?

The dilettante needs a serious wake-up call.

If a dilettante realizes that he's been outsmarted by his own Persona, he has a chance to get out of the trap by focusing solely on one activity. The dilettante also needs to understand the power of time and how committing at least ten years to one activity will bring not only great creative results, but also real personal growth—which is good. The dilettante's greatest fear (change) is the gift he should look forward to finding, not the thing to avoid.

NOTE: Here you may ask, *"But what if I'm not a dilettante, but a Renaissance man (or woman)?"* The answer is easy: If you're in fact a true Renaissance man (or woman), it means that you are simultaneously one of the best in the world in every category you touch (as a reference, see Da Vinci, who was the real deal). Is this you? If not—just slow down. Pick your best skill and focus on it for at least ten years. Keep the other stuff as hobbies. That's cool, too.

OBSTACLE 5: FAULTY PERCEPTION

The psychiatrist (and genius) **Carl Jung** made an incredibly powerful observation, by saying:

"Perception is projection."

This is a very important statement.

"Perception is projection" means that everything we see is always tainted by our own biases. We can never see reality as it truly is. Instead, we project our ideas of what things (or people) should be, and oddly, we also want them to stay the way we had envisioned. As you can imagine, this mechanic of "projecting" is driven by the Persona.

Because the Persona—in order to exist—always wants the original Personal Creation Story to be "right," we never see reality as it is. Instead, we see reality as the Persona wants us to see it.

In a sense, we are living in a world of illusions.

In intimate relationships, this is a common phenomenon. You meet someone new and project on this person a list of wonderful qualities you want him/her to have. Next thing you know, you are now in love with this imaginary "ideal" that you've just invented. With time, once the person turns out to be just human—with human flaws—you become angry at him/her for not conforming to your original projection/creation: *"What?! Why can't you be more the way I imagined you to be?!"* (I hope you can see the humor of the situation.)

In the realm of creativity, "perception is projection" can show up in two extremes, negative and positive—again, driven by the Persona.

> **Negative:** *"I can never succeed with this."*
> **Positive:** *"Piece of cake! This is so easy!"*

Both projections (positive or negative) can have a terrible impact. Let's start with the negative. By saying, *"I can never succeed with this,"* you obviously prevent yourself from trying—even if you could actually succeed.

The positive projection isn't better: *"Piece of cake! This is so easy!"* is an overconfident statement that can reflect a superficial understanding of a situation or a creative problem. And as it turns out, reality has very little patience for the underprepared.

So, how do we escape from "perception is projection"?

First, understand that the projection is directly related to your

Persona. The more the Persona is active, the more what you see is filtered through its lens, through various interpretations. If you're actively working on dissolving your Persona by using awareness, this is a great start.

Next, a smart way to move beyond projection is to approach any new project with a **beginner's mind**, saying, *"I know that I don't know."* This is important, especially if you are a seasoned professional in your field. Refrain from making the assumption that you know everything before the project begins. Be curious and stay open to discovery as you go into your project.

This is the humble approach. With a new creative project (or anything new in your life), try to keep your eyes and ears opened to what actually is (not what you want things to be). To do so, enlist other talents and ask them for feedback. Listen to what they say, and try to see things from multiple perspectives.

Please note that most people are naturally inclined to tell you what they think you want them to say. So watch out . . .

Let's imagine you want to open a retail location. Don't say:

> *"I'm about to sign this amazing space. I'm really excited about it. Do you see anything wrong with this?"*

With this type of question, you'll never get interesting feedback. Instead, say:

> *"Imagine this were your project. What would you look for in a retail location? What would make it attractive? What would be a deal-breaker for you?"*

That way, you'll get better, more meaningful feedback.

Another way to have a clearer view and avoiding personal projections is to make sure you do proper research in advance (see Part 3) by testing your project on its intended audience. Find people who could be the ideal audience and have them experience your project. If they struggle with it, don't correct them—accept what is and revise your project instead.

OBSTACLE 6: RATIONAL EXCUSES

Using "reason" in order to avoid moving forward with a creative project is an almost perfect trap. After all, how can anyone argue against a good ol' rational explanation?

As a creative person, you might have to deal with rational excuses both personally (from within), and professionally (from without: with clients, working relationships, etc.). Here, we're going to look at a common, and highly rational, excuse: the lack of money (another common one is "lack of time"—both use the same structure).

But before we go into it, please know that this type of excuse needs to be confronted as intensely as possible. Here's why:

In the entire history of humanity, nothing creative was ever accomplished because it was rational. Nothing.

Being creative is never a rational choice. Doing a creative project is never rational either. Attempting to create something new outside of the status quo cannot be rational—because there's always a risk with anything creative and new. That's a given.

And, of course, while you want to be smart and work with calculated risks (and we'll talk about that in Part 3), the risk is always there. In any case, the authentic creative gesture must be daring—not rational. It must also be intense.

The real question is, *"How much do you want it?"* Because if you want to realize something bad enough, you can always find the resources you need. Here, I'm going to give you a few examples.

It's the intensity, the vision, and the smarts that count. When you have these, your creativity can bend reality.

Examples:

No Computer, No Problem
I started working very young, at around age nineteen. And back in the day, computers that were powerful enough to do high-resolution imagery were not readily available (I'm that old). These machines used to cost over $100,000, and in Paris, where I grew up, they were rare. Only a handful of companies had them.

I obviously didn't have that kind of money, and I didn't have any contacts. But I absolutely wanted to work on these machines. For me, this was a priority. I was obsessed with this idea.

So here's what I did: One by one, I contacted each of these companies, and I visited them with my portfolio (which contained mostly hand-drawn visual ideas—ideas I had worked on for months). I asked these companies to let me work on their machines at night. I was very intense about it—because I would not let them say no. Two companies ended up accepting. And that's how I started.

For more than a year, I learned everything by working at night. My skin became translucent white. The night shift was gruesome and lonely. But it was worth it. After this period, I started working as a freelance graphic artist for an excellent fee because I was one of the few designers in Paris who could actually work on these machines. And years later, this allowed me to save money to buy my first computer (a Mac).

Great Storytelling

The acclaimed French product designer Ora Ito had been kicked out of his design school because he could not pay the tuition. Next, he tried to find internships to no avail; he was too young, too inexperienced. The reality in product design at the time was that, in order to create a prototype, you had to create very expensive molds (3-D printing did not exist yet). He also did not have access to the software he needed.

What he did was brilliant. First, he made a deal with someone he knew who had the software so he could get access to it. Next, he created 3-D renderings of his ideas. And, finally, he organized his ideas around unique storytelling about his vision (he's a master storyteller—see Part 3). Instead of showing these works to the design world (which had previously rejected him), he shared his stories with a new audience: the fashion world. They loved it. The press coverage he received attracted his first design clients. The rest is history.

From T-shirts to Fashion Empire

Gildas Loaec, co-founder of the luxury fashion brand and music label Maison Kitsuné, which has stores around the world, started with a couple of T-shirts. But his T-shirts were so unique they commanded attention. His selling strategy was *"You need this if you want to be contemporary."* His conviction in his vision was so firm, so intense, that it influenced buyers. In the span of ten years, this intensity propelled his brand into the luxury world. He and his business partner have accomplished this feat without initial financial backup.

Lack of Time

"I don't have any time!" cried my friend Kristen. *"I'm a mom; I have no time for myself."* No one can argue with this statement . . . but . . . could she find a creative way to make time for herself? I asked Kristen to create a log journal and describe every activity that was taking place in her life—and yes, she was in fact, very busy. But we were able to create time by making two simple tweaks. First, by asking for support. Because Kristen was doing everything herself, she was drained mentally and physically. It took her some courage, but she asked for help: Once a week, her friend Olivia came over to babysit the kids; in exchange, Kristen helped her with bookkeeping. And three times a week, her husband was in charge of making dinner. Next, the daily two hours of nighttime TV was replaced with personal time for her project. These simple tweaks gave her the time she needed.

. . .

These are, of course, just a few examples. And today, the obstacles that you may face are obviously unique to your own experience. But please never let rational excuses prevent you from pursuing your creative dreams.

Any rational excuse (lack of funds, lack of time, lack of experience) can be counterbalanced with your intensity, your vision, and your smarts (see Part 3).

Your creative gesture must be defiant. It's your job to

brainstorm and find creative ways around any obstacle in order to realize your vision. That's how Creative Dreaming works.

Remember, in the Creative Dreaming Method, we look at decades onward. If you want to realize your dream and every day for the next ten years you work intelligently in that direction, you will succeed. And in doing so, you will also create a beautiful life—a real adventure.

My creative friend, I know you have the capacity to be bold, and defiant when you want to. Channel this energy into your project—commit to it—and soon, you'll start seeing remarkable results.

OBSTACLE 7: THE THIRST FOR QUICK VALIDATION
"Results! Results! Results! I need good results, now!"

The most interesting creative people are always the most sensitive. When you have developed an uncommon talent or a skill—your strength also comes with a weakness.

This weakness is a desire for outside validation (which is closely related to Obstacle 3.2).

Wanting immediate results is dangerous because—on the surface—it appears to be connected with your "drive" to create successfully. In reality, it's a distracting poison that can prevent you from growing long-term.

This thirst is directly related to the Persona, which says, *"I need instant outside validation to know that what I'm doing will give me the ideal outcome I want. If not, it means I'm a failure."*

This is again the Persona's faulty logic at work. No one is a failure for attempting something creative and not getting immediate positive feedback!

In fact, your capacity to keep creating and evolving over the years is what is making you a creative success, today (please note the present tense). I've talked before about the concept of mastery to highlight this idea:

Being a creative success is not a destination. It's an ongoing process—it's what you're doing today to grow and evolve.

Here, I need to clarify one thing; results are indeed important, because in order to be successful with any creative project, you'll need to act and get feedback. We get it. Without feedback, it's impossible to know where you stand.

But what we're talking about here is something else entirely. We're talking about the thirst for outside validation through "results"—which has nothing to do with drive or with getting feedback. It's very important to see the difference.

The desire for validation can become intoxicating, and addictive—like a high. And today, because of social media (and how it works by accounting for the numbers of "likes" and followers), this addiction is global.

The problem goes like this: If your only goal is to get instant outside validation, it's more likely that you'll end up doing what everyone else is doing. In the short term, it might work. In the long term, it's a killer. When your work is derivative, it has no real value.

In reality, if your work is truly innovative, your audience might need some time to catch up with you.

This is why, when you are asked, *"How do I become successful creatively?"* the classic answer always is: *"Be yourself. Develop your own voice."* While this advice is true, it's easier said than done. Developing your own voice takes time. It takes courage. It takes patience.

This is extremely important: As a creative, you should have a sense of self that is never connected with the immediate results you're getting, or not getting—because ultimately this is something outside of your control.

Anyone who is successful creatively will go through ups and downs throughout his/her career. That's part of life.

For you to be able to work successfully for decades to come, your validation should always come from within. Your job is to focus on your process.

Your only goal should be to create your own, self-contained creative loop, which will generate its own reward (See Part 3.):

- First, research, imagine, and create.
- Second, release, promote, and get feedback.
- Third, learn from feedback, adjust, and grow.
- Repeat.

OBSTACLE 8: POOR TIMING

The relationship between time and creativity is an incredibly fascinating subject that could fill another book (If you haven't already, please check out my TEDx talk "How to Create the

Future" on YouTube for some wild time-hacking adventures). Time being both elastic, and subjective, you can find yourself in a situation where you are either "always short on time" or "have too much time on your hands."

Because your ability to master time is directly related to your creative success, the Persona loves to use it against you by using, once again, unawareness.

This is really easy to spot and to fix.

> • If your Persona is rushing you, saying, *"We need this right now, or else!"* then, slow down and recenter. Take the time to focus on what really matters.

> • If your Persona says, *"Take all the time you need; follow your process,"* and by following this (apparently sound) advice, you're realizing that you've been working on the first thirty pages of your novel for the last ten years, then it's time to whip yourself into action! Challenge yourself to finish your project by a specific deadline.

To bring awareness to your relationship with time, an interesting approach is to look at your own life as a series of decades.

Here, **Bill Gates**'s advice comes to mind:

"We always overestimate the change that will occur in the next two years and underestimate the change that will occur in the next ten."

To paraphrase the great Bill, it means, for us creatives, that we tend to overestimate what we can do in a year (or even six months), and we underestimate what we can achieve in ten years.

I'm sure you've heard of the ten-year rule, right?

Popularized by **Malcolm Gladwell** in his 2008 book, *Outliers*, the idea states that in order to achieve mastery in any skill you need to put 10,000 hours into it. This is about twenty hours every week for ten years (or 2.8 hours, every day).

So, do you have 2.8 hours every day?
If not, you must create this space for yourself.

If you want to get uncommon results, you need to start an uncommon relationship with time.

A way to start thinking about this in your own life is to realize that your most precious asset is, in fact, time. Once you truly get this, it becomes your number one priority and you can figure out ways to create more time for yourself.

Time management is a life-hacking skill—every case is unique. Here's a list of some of the things I do to create time in my life (and this process took years to fine-tune).

These examples are not meant to be duplicated; they're just here to help you think about your own relationship with time.

My time strategy works in two directions. First, I'm saving time with Time Savers, so I can later enjoy all the time I want in activities I call Time Expanders.

Time Savers:
– Removing all time wasters (things and people) that don't contribute to my creative well-being and/or real happiness.
– Learning to say "no" to (fake) opportunities that are not supporting my creative goals. Sometimes, it's hard to figure them out intellectually, so I trust my gut instinct. If it doesn't feel right, I pass.
– No TV in the house. Ever.
– Social media: less than twenty minutes per day.
– Cutting my own hair (this is a weird habit, but an incredible time saver).
– Waking up every day around 6:30 a.m. (I never thought I could do this; now it's a routine).
– Preparing everything in advance. From the clothes to wear, the food to eat, or to-do lists, everything is ready for the next day. Upon waking up—it's go time.
– Trading money for time. In the way I get paid, I'd rather get paid a bit less if I have more time in return. This is a newer concept for me that had allowed me (paradoxically) to actually earn more in the long term than I used to (because I'm using this free time to create income-generating projects)!
– Getting help with tasks I'm not good at. I have a super team of bookkeeper and accountant, because these tasks are not my favorites.
– Living within my means. Getting rid of stuff. It's not just that by "owning too many things, these things end up owning you," as the saying goes; it's that they also demand your time. I used to own an adorable vintage 1984 Porsche 911 that needed constant maintenance—I happily sold it, with no regrets. Lifestyle doesn't bring creative happiness or long-term results (see Obstacle 9). Less is more.
– No multitasking. If I'm with my family, I'm 100 percent with them—I don't answer business e-mails while we're together.

When I work, I'm entirely focused on one task only.
– Chunking. I work through lengths of 90 minutes of full focus (while my phone is away). Then, I take a 10-minute break before going back to work. I'm an extreme monotasker; and it's a discipline I've had to learn the hard way because I'm also ADHD. Focusing on just one thing allows me to produce more in less time.

And finally, my favorite . . .

– Beating the crowd, every time (never being in traffic). I used to live in Los Angeles, where traffic is a real issue—unless, of course, you're out-of-sync with everyone else. It's a fun habit to work on. This means that, on the weekends, we would go to the beach very early, then would go shopping, before everyone. We would go see movies early or very late. And dinners out would always be either weekdays or Sundays (never on the dreaded Fridays, or Saturdays, aka "Amateur Nights"). You get it—live out-of-sync, and you'll never complain about traffic ever again.

These time savers allow me a lot of space where I can take as much time as I want.

Time Expanders:
– I love driving my daughter to school with my wife in the morning.
– Late-night conversations with my wife.
– Conversations with friends.
– Writing.
– Reading.
– Teaching (I often go overtime in my classes—this is not a problem because I love teaching so much).
– Creating.

– Learning new skills.
– Building wood furniture.
– Hiking.

I'm sharing this with you only to get you to think about time. It's not what I do that counts—it's what you can do.

Getting the right rhythm in your own life is a learned skill. It's also really fun to play with it. You can experiment with numerous little time hacks throughout your day—and the next thing you know, you'll have freed three hours for your creative work.

Take a serious look at time in your life—what could be changed?

OBSTACLE 9: FALLING FOR THE EXTREMES OF LIFESTYLE

The lifestyle trap is directly related to Obstacle 3 (The Desire for Perfection), and it's one of the trickiest obstacles to go around. Lifestyle is tricky because, as you'll see, you can't dismiss it entirely. It's one of these things that can be a hindrance to your creative life, *or* an advantage.

So here, I'll present multiple perspectives, and based on your own life, you'll know where to position yourself.

First, what is lifestyle?

Lifestyle is a form of creative storytelling (often used on social media) that shows your life in the everyday. It can be a behind-the-scenes video, a studio or house tour, travels, a work-in-progress, etc. It can also include personal moments—when you're not working.

Lifestyle stories help your audience get to know you.

In itself, there's nothing wrong with lifestyle—unless it's pushed to the extreme. Then, lifestyle becomes a trap because it becomes your only creative goal.

Let me explain.

What we've been talking about in this book is the authentic creative gesture, a transformative power.

Through your creative act, you are evolving and bringing in the new. In doing so, you are altering how you spend your days and the way you live. Slowly but surely, through the everyday sacrifices of your ongoing creative process, a new "you" arises, a new identity.

The creative process is the identity you create.

For true creatives, what this identity looks like on the outside is not that important. For example, if you're wearing overalls because you work with clay or you dye fabric—and it's messy— you're not wearing your outfit because it's going to make you "look cool." You wear it because it's practical. What counts is the quality of your work and how you express yourself. What's cool is your process, not your pants.

Now, wait! There's a major problem!

As I've shared with you in the opening chapter of this book, in today's world, "being creative" is now considered "cool." Interestingly, this is a very recent development; before, creative types were always looked at with a mix of envy and suspicion.

But now, everything has changed. And as it turns out, "cool" has also become the most precious currency in marketing (the business of selling).

This creates the perfect storm that allows the dark side of lifestyle to come creeping in. And it offers a devilish proposition:

Lifestyle is the identity you can buy.

Lifestyle says: *"Why make the grueling efforts associated with creative life when instead you can buy the 'right look,' and get the same results?"*

A true deal with the devil, indeed.

The lifestyle trend started in the late 1960s, and exploded in the 1970s. You can discover it in the editorial and advertising pages of old issues of the granddaddy of lifestyle in the U.S.— *Playboy* magazine. There, you'll find suggestions that by simply buying a camera, a fancy sports car, or a new stereo, you will live a "perfect," happy, worry-free hedonistic life. You'll have status; you will become a sex symbol. By acquiring and surrounding yourself with material goods to project the image of success, you will be successful.

All you need to know is *what* to buy.

While this dream of "happiness through consumption" turned out to be an empty promise—and a trap— for the previous generations who indulged in it, it's still very much alive in the twenty-first century.

Today, this search for a "perfect," imaginary life has dramatically increased by entering a new playground: social media.

Under the guise of "discovering an artist's process to make a meaningful connection with the audience"—which sounds totally fine—social media has instead created millions of "lifestyle artists" who "look the part" as they are seemingly living the creative life through beautifully curated pictures.

But in reality, these lifestylers have pushed it to an extreme. They spend more time "looking creative"—by spending money to look creative—than actually doing anything creative.

You can find these lifestyle artists in every category you can think of: contemporary arts, photography, design, craft, fashion, illustration, cooking, music, yoga, fitness, etc.

Lifestylers are everywhere.

Because social media favors lifestyle stories, lifestylers tend to get a lot of followers. And because they have lots of followers, they get the attention of brands for collaborations. Shockingly—it works!

But this shortcut always has a hidden price.

Getting positive feedback because you dress the part, live in an incredible loft, travel around the world, or use expensive equipment is never a shortcut to answering this question:

How authentic is your work?

And this is where it gets brutal. Because they are entrapped by their own image, many lifestylers can't produce meaningful work. In addition, they also live in permanent fear, worrying that this image they have created might not be "right."

Lifestylers are living a lie—and paying the price for it. On the outside, their public image is always picture-perfect: They brag about how happy they are; they constantly point at the latest gadgets they own and the expensive vacations they indulge in. Yet, on the inside, they are plagued by anxiety. Lifestyle, pushed to the extreme, becomes an addiction that demands every financial resource available.

Lifestylers look great in pictures, but—and this is their darkest, most private secret—most of them are financially broke. They spend beyond their means in the pursuit of their perfect image.

The folly of the lifestyler is directly connected to the Persona, which demands that you conform to a perfect image. Lifestyle, taken to an extreme, forces you to follow an artificial, rigid image that dictates what you should look like and what you should say. It's an image-prison that prevents you from exploring real creativity.

In contrast, the authentic creative life is a liberating process. And each creative project builds creative equity in your own life: a transformation on the outside, and on the inside as well.

Creativity allows you to experience the freedom to grow through self-expression. And this freedom—which you get to actually experience—gives you something truly unique: the genuine glow of happiness.

Pushed to an extreme, lifestyle is trap. A complex trap.

There's a running joke in photography that describes it perfectly. It goes like this:

> *"If you're unhappy with your photographs,*
> *the solution is always to buy more gear!"*

This is, obviously, a fool's game.

An amazing $50,000 camera might be the right tool for some specific projects (yes, this exists—check out Hasselblad cameras), but it will not make you a better photographer. Nor will an amazing loft space make you create better paintings. Nor will a new hair color make you a better singer.

Lifestyle doesn't make the artist—it's the other way around.

So if you're tempted to spend on expensive gear because you may think that lifestyle will make you a better creative, don't fall for that trap. Instead, follow your process by creating amazing projects with the tools you currently have (see Part 3).

Yet . . . there's another major twist. So hang on.

Lifestyle cannot be entirely discarded—and that's an interesting paradox.

In Part 3, I'm going to talk about promoting your work. And lifestyle is actually a part of it.

You see, too much lifestyle will kill your creative life. Too little will do the same.

Unlike Lifestylers, many creatives actually fall for another extreme: They refuse to promote their work, adopting the "I'm an hermit," holier-than-thou strategy.

Not good.

This approach is dangerous because no matter what your creative project is, it always needs to be in relationship with an audience. If you say, *"I'll just do great work, and I'll be discovered,"* then you live in fantasy. Today—no matter how great you are—you actively need to promote yourself so your work can find its audience. And your job is not done until you do that.

How do you promote yourself?

One of the most effective ways to do so is (get ready) . . .

lifestyle!

See . . . I told you there was a twist.

And here, it simply means sharing your process to make a meaningful connection with your audience. Interestingly, it doesn't need to be glamorous—keep it real. What's important is your storytelling.

If you work in a tiny space, show it. If your studio area is next to noisy neighbors, show your noise-canceling headphones. Make your daily struggles and your little successes an epic adventure. Enlist your audience by showing them that you're an unstoppable creative force.

Conclusion 1: Lifestyle is tricky. Too much (or too little) lifestyle becomes a trap that can kill your creative life. Use it within reason. Make sure that the storytelling you are creating serves your creative freedom and self-expression, first.

Conclusion 2 (and one final twist): There's one rare exception to the lifestyle trap. *If*—and that's a big, giant "if"—your superpower (see Part 3) is being a natural lifestyle artist because that's what you do creatively, and, *if* you truly stand out in this category because you have a unique voice, then go for it. Express your superpower.

OBSTACLE 10: LIFE'S HARDSHIPS
Here, we're going to end this chapter with a delicate subject. I'm going to talk with you about something that no one wants to talk about: life's real hardships.

Life's hardships can touch us all. Good people can get sick and die; accidents can strike; tragedies can unfold . . .

This happens every day, and as we all know, this is how things are. Life is made of polarities; the good and the bad happen all at once. One cannot exist without the other.

Sometimes you can get hit really hard—randomly. For no reason. And, if this happens to you, you'll often have to deal with it alone. Why? Because life's hardships are the scariest things to contemplate for humans. We tend to hide from them— because if not, we foolishly believe we might catch some bad juju in the process (a perfect example of the Persona's faulty logic at work).

And now, I'd like to share with you a perspective. And this, my creative friend, is coming from someone who's been through his share of Life's challenges. Some were of the kind that were considered "unconquerable," but they were indeed conquered.

Here it is . . .

If Life has thrown something at you (no matter how big and devastating), it's your job as a human being to get back on your feet—no matter what. And it might take years, decades even. But it doesn't matter. You need to find the resolve within your own soul to move yourself back up—especially if everyone agrees that this is impossible.

The larger the challenge, the more you'll hear hints that it's okay for you to give up. *"She went through hell, so it's understandable that she can't . . ."* is the type of comment that's pure poison. It may sound like a caring voice, but it has the opposite effect.

You must never give up. This is not an option. You, my creative friend, must never give up. *Never.*

Instead, you must use your creativity and adapt.

"If you're going through hell, keep going," said **Winston Churchill** during World War II, while England was under attack by Nazi Germany. He was right. You must fight for your own life and keep at it, one step at a time. Always.

Here's an important part of this: If you need time to get back on your feet, make that your creative project. Take as much time as you need, even if you think you don't have any.

Bend time.

You might "lose everything," but if you connect with your True Self—your creative core—you can find the power to "go through anything." Make each completed day a victory—and slowly build on it. Embrace every hour of living as a gift. Because it is a gift.

Be patient. As long as you're committed to being fully aware of what's happening, you will grow. You need to know that, no matter what you're facing, there is always hope. Even if it takes a form that you would never have considered before.

Stay open.

If you're ready to bring your full radiance, and live every single day you have in front of you with complete intensity—even if the days are counted (and in the big picture, they always are), something will be given.

Every time Life takes something away, it gives something back. That's always the deal with Life. This is true even when we are confronted with real tragedy. But awareness is key—being fully present must be your sole priority.

Here, I want to be really clear: What I'm talking about is not a quick fix to avoid trouble, pain, or suffering. Awareness means allowing what is to unfold, and that includes the bad stuff. But once you have full awareness, once you're fully present, something is given that can help you grow through the experience.

This is hard to describe . . . The pain is the same, the experience is as traumatic, and there's obviously no guarantee of any desired outcome.

But when you bring full awareness to what *is*, you enter into a new relationship with Life.

You start understanding that the polarities of Life (the good and the bad) have a real purpose. And once you align yourself with that purpose by being present—once you're fully engaged with it by finding the complete resolve to making your life (and becoming) the expression of courage, resiliency, and strength— something will be given.

The pain of loss (including of loved ones) is directly related to the amount of love that's in your heart. The suffering is connected to the richness of your love. And this love can never be taken away from you.

When you become fully aware of this fact by experiencing it, you will feel what I can only attempt to describe as "the shine of grace." You will be changed. You will find the treasure that Life has in store for all of us.

You will experience that Life (with a big "L") is Love (with a big "L")—the transcendent Love that burns through space and time. The Love eternal that connects us all.

Once this happens, every single day will reveal the fullness hidden in your own life. By experiencing it, you will become truly alive.

. . .

This, my creative friend, is my message to you if you're confronted by Life's real hardships. I hope it helps.

YOU DID IT!
This is it!

Together, we've been through the toughest lines I've ever written about creativity—I've left no stone unturned—and you're still in one piece! I've challenged you in every possible way, and you've survived.

Congrats, my creative friend. *You* did it!

Part 1 and Part 2 are behind us—and the hard conversation is over. You now have a map to look at reality and your place in it from a new perspective. You can now see how your creative process is directly related to the creation of your self. And finally—inside or out—you are prepared to deal with any obstacles that your creative life will throw at you.

You are ready.

In Part 3, I'm going to share very specific tactics and strategies of the Creative Dreaming method to imagine and realize your ideas in the real world.

This is the final part of our journey.

We're finally ready for action.

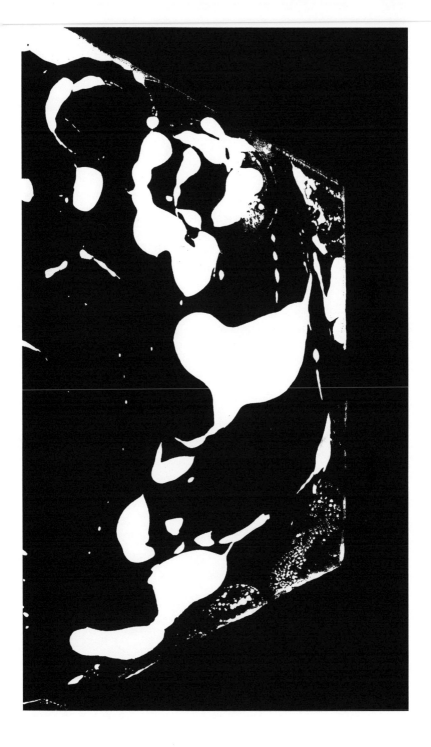

**The Game of Life is constantly challenging
you to grow and evolve.**

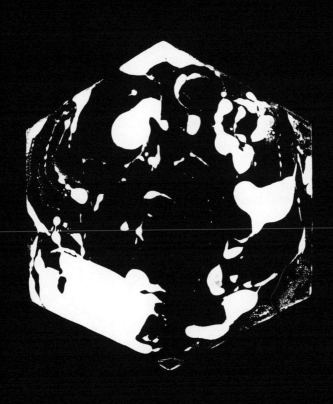

Your creative life is an obstacle game you're creating to achieve the satisfaction of growing, evolving, and experiencing freedom.

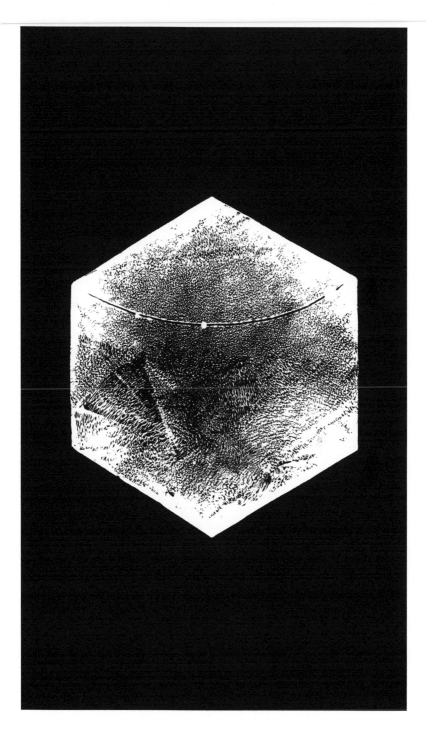

**You have to be defiant with Life.
Joyfully defiant.**

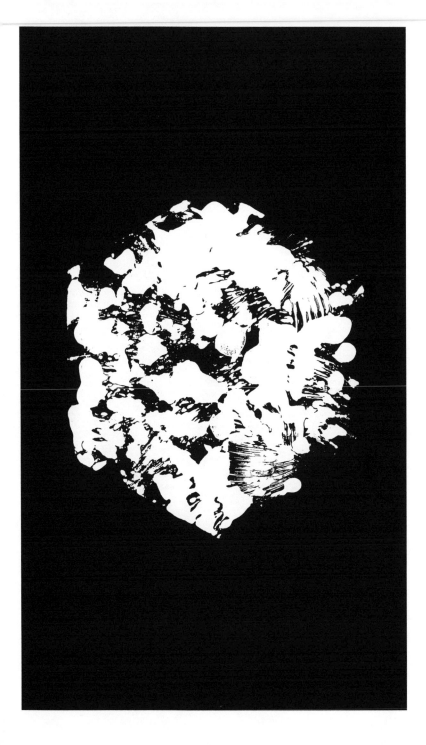

Mastery is the unfolding of your True Self through your creative expression.

The movement of your True Self is set toward awareness, creativity, discovery, aliveness, character, and determination.

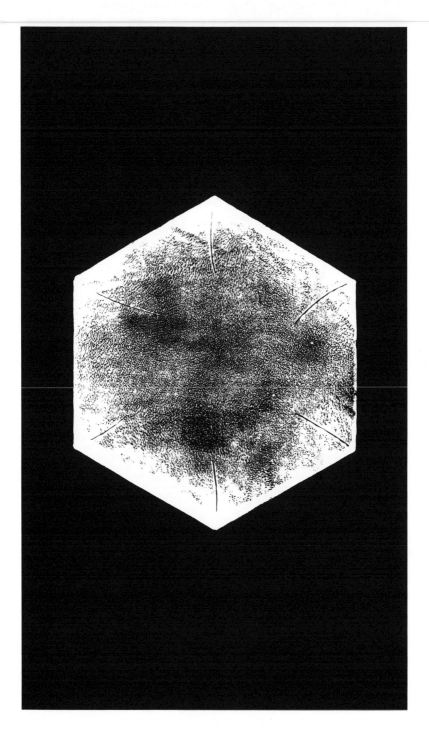

Being a creative success
is not a destination.
The gift of your creative life
is the process itself.

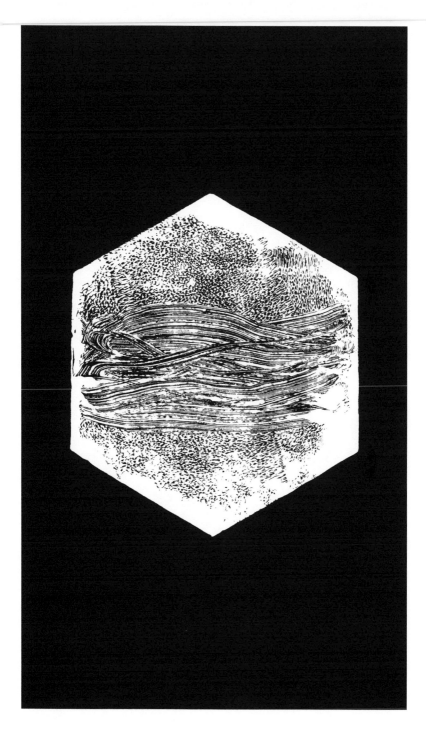

"What you truly want" is the knowledge
that arises in the present by interacting with
reality. The experience of life hides the gem.

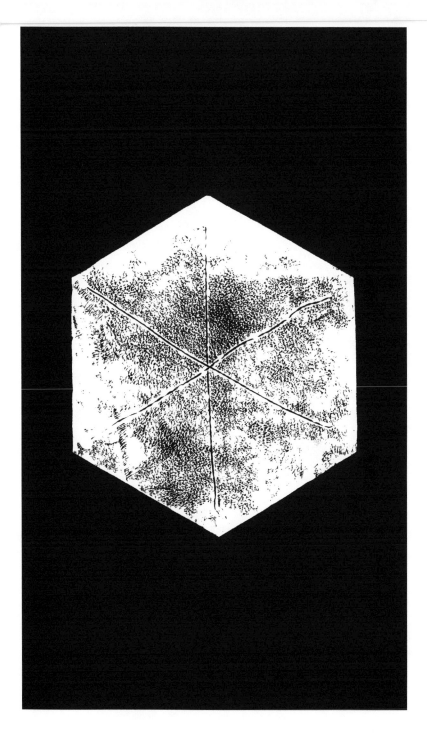

When you bring full awareness to what is,
you enter into a new relationship with Life.

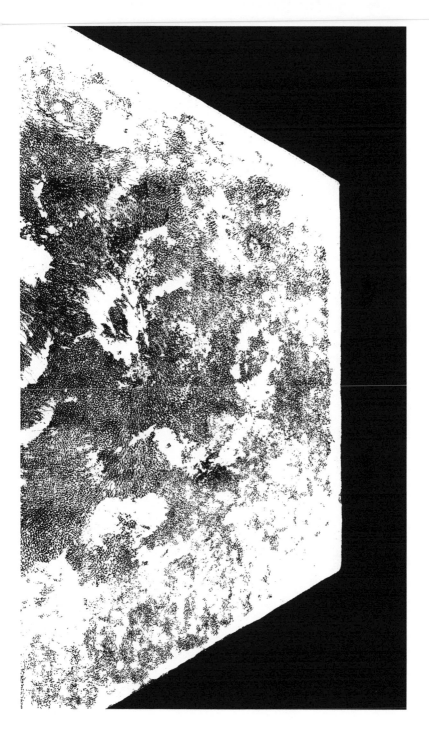

PART 3

CREATIVE

DREAMING

DREAM WITH CERTAINTY

Welcome to Part 3. Here we're going to get tactical. Our map is now ready—it's time to create.

In this section, I'm going to walk you through a process, as if we were in a workshop together. I'm going to ask you questions, and I'll invite you to write your answers in the book. This process will give you clarity on the steps you'll need to take to achieve your creative dream.

As we go through these steps together, please keep this concept in mind: Your dream is not only possible, it's within your reach.

You can dream with certainty.

How come? Because, my creative friend, the creative greatness in your own life is never something that happens by accident.

Whether you decide to create a company, start a creative project, change your career, have a fantastic family life, cultivate great relationships, contribute to society, or live a vibrant, healthy life—nothing ever happens randomly. Your creative success is the byproduct of the relationship you've established with Life: It's an ongoing practice, backed up by effective tactical strategies.

Together, in the previous chapters, we've first established a guiding model for reality/self that is focused on growth. Now that it has been set up, we can move forward and act, in order to get feedback.

THE BIG VISUALIZATION

Now we're going to start by creating a big vision for your own life. I'm going to ask you to think about your dream.

Imagine that you have realized it.

Imagine yourself, five years from now. Imagine that you have created the life you wanted.

No limitations . . .

Ideally, what does it look like?

What does your day look like?

Where do you live?

What does your house look like?

Who are the people you are sharing your life with?

What do you do for fun?

How do you feel?

How do you look?

Stay in this image for a few seconds. Good.

Now let's continue. You are in this new world, five years from now. You're enjoying this beautiful life that you have created.

And yes, it's truly amazing, because it's not someone else's dream. It's truly yours. You've just had a great day. You feel great. You look great.

It's the end of the day, and as you walk in your house you catch your reflection in the bathroom mirror. You look different. You have the glow that comes with being fully present.

"So many things have changed," you think. *"I have changed so much in the past few years."*

And now you start thinking about your past. You start thinking about the person you were back then, when you were just learning about the Creative Dreaming Method.

You smile and think:

"What advice could I give to my past self?

Who did I become, in order to achieve my beautiful dream?

What did I allow myself to experience?

Where did I go outside my comfort zone?

What new skills did I learn?

What habits did I let go of?

What project did I finally start that became the vehicle for all this change to happen?

What steps did I take?"

And now let's return to the present moment.

Interesting exercise, isn't it?

By answering these questions in your own life and, every single day, building stepping stones toward this future, you will make it real.

You see, by traveling in your imagination to your desired dream, you can actually learn a lot about what you need to do in the present moment to make this dream come true.

This idea of connecting with your future self, and retracing the steps that lead to this outcome, is fascinating.

The process is a bit mysterious. How does it work?

In order to learn more about the power of visualization and goals, we are now going to look into time.

TIME HACKING
As we discovered in our conversation together, the past is very much alive in the present. And we see it at work through the Persona.

This implies that time is a living relationship.

Instead of the classic horizontal timeline that we've learned about in school—a line that goes from past, to present, to future—we need a new model.

In our interactions with the Persona, we see that the past is always fused with the present, as one unit. But if in fact time is a living relationship, then the future is always fused with the present as well.

Therefore, in the Creative Dreaming Method, we use a model that looks at time as an ongoing, cohesive unit—where past, present, and future are in a living relationship.

Past, present, and future—as one living sphere.

This radical approach to envisioning time is not a fantasy. In fact, two of the most important scientists and visionaries of the twentieth century have described it in such a way.

Albert Einstein declared, *"The distinction between the past, present, and future is only a stubbornly persistent illusion."*

And **David Bohm** went even deeper, by saying, *"In any given period of time the whole of time may be enfolded. . . . One moment of time contains information about all of it."*

And now you might be wondering, *"But why is it important to think about time?"*
It's because this new understanding of time explains why goal visualization is so important to making your dreams come true.

It just works.

FOUR STEPS TO YOUR DREAM
In the Creative Dreaming Method, when we set up a dream/ goal, it's with the understanding that we fully intend to alter our future. I've shared with you before this idea of "dreaming with certainty."

You are not here to dive into a fantasy world—on the contrary—your goal is to hack your reality. You want to create real change.

In the previous visualization exercise where you've met with your future self, the most important aspect is to figure out the steps you need to take to get to this desired future. This is similar to what scientists call "reverse engineering." You start from the end and go backward, devising the steps needed until you come back to where you are today.

Some of the steps will involve external activities (such as creating a specific project or learning new skills), but other steps will demand inner transformation.

But here, your intent is key.

External or internal, you have to laser-focus on these steps —with the absolute resolve to make them happen.

Taking these steps should become an absolute must for you, no matter what.

Every time you are going to imagine and visualize a new dream, you will be challenged by Life. That's how it works. Because a dream—to be of value—will always challenge your comfort zone.

In the Creative Dreaming Method, we have been talking about the defiant stance. This is your absolute willingness to take the steps, the resolve to work on your process.

Here are the four steps to successful visualization:

1. Imagine something beautiful and inspiring. A future in which your life has changed and a future in which you have changed as well. Explore this vision. Feel it.

2. From this vision of the future, look back to where you are today. One by one, track back the steps that are needed until you reach where you are now. Make sure that you work simultaneously on external and internal steps.

3. Every single day, work on these steps, one by one. Plow through the resistance, the setbacks, the delays, and the disappointments. Adjust and adapt. Keep going.

4. Revise your process, and grow from it.

SMALL DAILY VISUALIZATIONS

I've started sharing with you how to visualize a big dream, realized five years from now. I've also showed you how to tap into this future reality to find clues about the steps you can take today. But the practice of visualization can also be used for smaller key moments.

- Before you go to bed, you can visualize and mentally rehearse what you intend to accomplish the next day.
- Before an important meeting, you can visualize the entire interaction.
- Before a trip, you can visualize every step involved.
- Before you start working, you can visualize how you will execute a specific task.
- Before a test or a performance, you can visualize yourself focused in that moment.

You can use this practice in every aspect of life.

These small, daily visualizations allow your brain to rehearse an event in advance. In doing so, you'll find out that you might discover elements that you could improve beforehand. This will also give you peace of mind: Once the event takes place, you'll feel confident and prepared.

The more you practice visualization with a specific intent, the more engaged you will be with reality—even if things don't turn out exactly the way you planned.

Try this practice on a small scale. Your engagement with life and the results you'll get will soar naturally.

TACTICAL CREATIVE DREAMING
Now that we've explored how to tap into our imagination to visualize future dreams, we are now going to get into the specific steps to make our dreams come true.

In the following sections, we are going to use tactical strategies to create a creative project from beginning to end. This approach can be used to create a new business, begin a creative practice, learn new skills, or bring change into a specific domain of your life.

In this tactical phase, your first goal is to gain insight. This is achieved by cultivating your Three Creative Assets, an ongoing, lifelong process, designed to keep you growing and fill you up with fresh, creative ideas.

Once you have a true insight—a great idea—it's time to execute it through a specific campaign/project. To do so, you will use the Creative Dreaming Tactical Blueprint.

THE SECRET TO CREATIVE DREAMING IS INSIGHT
Let's look at our Principles 3 and 4:

3. Everything is interconnected. From micro to macro, everything works together. The small influences the big. The big influences the small.

4. Every complex living system only exists in relationship to the Whole. The Whole is made of the many. The many is a reflection of the Whole.

Any idea or dream you'd like to create always needs to exist in relationship with the Whole. And as the creator of this idea, your creative greatness is always the byproduct of the ongoing relationship taking place between you, your idea, and your life (your audience, your category, and the world).

Imagine walking into the ocean and becoming one with it—this is what's actually happening, today, with your own life. You are standing in the Whole; you are a part of it.

The more you understand how all the parts of the Whole are working simultaneously and influencing each other, the more you'll be able to succeed creatively.

Yet there's a very important distinction: Knowing how everything works is not enough. Information—alone—has only limited value.

Here's the secret to Creative Dreaming: For your creative idea to be successful, your goal is to develop a real insight.

An insight simply means "the capacity to gain an accurate and deep understanding of a person or thing."

Quite often, this insight appears like a flash of inspiration after countless hours of gruesome effort. A flash that says: *"I know exactly what to do now. I know it's going to work."*

And it does.

I believe, my creative friend, that you've already experienced something similar in your life.

The insight always calls for something new. It often appears when there's the need for a change to occur in one's life, or in a field that has become saturated with the same ideas.

An insight can be translated into many shapes—ranging between two extremes: from evolution to revolution.

Evolution in Your Field
One of the simplest ways to create is to improve upon what already exists. What you offer is an evolution toward progress. Here, your insight can be a simple tweak that can have a great impact:

> • Practicing your skill in a new way or in a new context.
> • Offering your skill/product/experience to a new audience.
> • Taking what you do already onto a new platform (new media or market).
> • Offering the opposite of what everyone else is offering in your field.
> • Feeling when the audience is looking for a new direction in your field, and being the first one to offer it.

This approach, while gentle (and relatively safe), can pack a lot of punch—especially if it's applied on an ongoing basis. A lot of little tweaks can create something big.

Revolution in Your Field

Shock tactics and creative revolutions have real power. Here, you're making a bold move: You point at something publicly and you declare that it represents the past (this is old!). To replace it, you offer your insight—a radical, new vision of what the present should be like.

See, for example, Coco Chanel or Rei Kawakubo in fashion; Pablo Picasso or Andy Warhol in art; the French New Wave films; Malcolm McLaren and Vivienne Westwood with the Punk movement; David Bowie's glam rock Ziggy Stardust extravaganza in music; or Apple Computer's first years in business.

Unlike the previous method of evolution, this radical approach is tough—it actually takes real genius to pull it off. If you want to start a creative revolution in your field, you must be a real visionary and truly have substance. No matter what your insight is, you need to back it up with some hard truth. But if you're authentic, this approach can create some serious magic.

As you can see, your insight can express itself in different ways. Evolution and revolution are two paths to innovation and change. Start where you are today, and pick the one that's the right fit for you.

Once you have a real insight, you will be able to develop and express an opinion and articulate it through your message.

If your insight is real—and if you're able to present it strategically—you will succeed. In that sense, **the Creative Dreamer is always an insight-seeker.**

Here, my creative friend, you might be asking yourself, *"But how do I get this insight?"*

Simple.

You will get it by working on the ongoing Creative Dreaming process we're calling the Three Creative Assets.

And remember, even if you don't see results immediately (it takes time), your everyday practice equals success.

If you grow every day, you are being successful.

YOUR THREE CREATIVE ASSETS

While an infinite number of parts are working together in your life, in Creative Dreaming you only need to focus on three assets first, and keep growing them.

The Three Creative Assets

Your Mindset
Your Skills and Point of View
Your Message

YOUR MINDSET

Creative Dreaming is a radical approach to creating change. In Part 1 and Part 2, we started with a map that can help you get into the right mindset. Study this map thoroughly—and use it.

The Creative Dreaming mindset is extremely important—and

this is why we have dedicated two-thirds of the book to it. I hope I was able to convey that by radically altering your perspective, you can uncover the unseen and innovate.

But this is not all; to succeed with your creative project, finding an idea is not enough. You have to become an unstoppable force to actualize it into the world. And this is the most important mindset you must cultivate:

You have to be extremely clear with yourself and decide to become unstoppable, no matter what.

And as I mentioned before, this has nothing to do with being aggressive—you can be simultaneously kind and an unstoppable force—it's your resolve that counts.

Be joyfully defiant.

Before we continue, there's an important distinction I'd like to highlight. Many people think that to be unstoppable, you have to be stubborn. This is a big mistake.

You want to be an adaptive, unstoppable force.

If something isn't working, you must be flexible and try a different approach (more in the Tactical Blueprint). The more flexible you are, the more you can adapt to change, and therefore, the more you will succeed.

See our Principle 8.
8. Life is adaptive.

I really want you to remember this:

Be flexible as you dream. Always adapt to the new. Stay open to the possibilities that are right in front of you.

YOUR SKILLS AND POINT OF VIEW
Your Skills

Now, my creative friend, based on your flexible, unstoppable mindset, you are now ready to work on your skills.

And here, regardless of your field, there's only one approach: To grow your skills you need to get uncomfortable.

That's right.

And this has nothing to do with just the amount of work you're putting into it, or your personal history. Being willing to be uncomfortable is the opposite of entitlement. Let me explain:

Saying, *"I've worked on this for five hundred hours!"* and expecting recognition and success is total Persona B.S. (Boring Subterfuge).

Saying, *"I've struggled decades to become an artist!"* and—because of it—expecting recognition and success is, again, total Persona B.S. It's not quantity or personal merit (real or imagined); it's quality.

Every day, get out of your comfort zone. Quality ideas and quality work comes from your willingness to be uncomfortable, from your drive to explore the unknown. I feel that you know exactly what I'm talking about.

For a graphic designer, being uncomfortable means getting away from Adobe Creative Suite (and your computer) and instead, building a spatial installation in nature that could involve projection mapping (and learning how to make that happen).

For a weaver, getting uncomfortable means learning new weaving techniques you've never explored before, or new ways to dye materials. It could also mean learning storytelling and filmmaking to show your work in a new context—by, perhaps, connecting with a dance company and collaborating on a film.

For a chef, getting uncomfortable means getting in front of the camera and sharing your passion for food by using a narrative that has never been seen before. Or creating a one-of-a-kind experience that connects food and community.

For a photographer, getting uncomfortable means having the courage to go after difficult assignments, the ones you've been wanting to do all your life.

For an author or a lyricist, getting uncomfortable means telling something real. Telling the truth. Having the courage to be vulnerable instead of trying to do what you think the audience (or your manager/agent) wants.

For a fashion designer, getting uncomfortable means being authentic by moving beyond the surface of style and exploring meaning and culture. Being inspired by something and going deep by embodying it as well, in your own life. Doing this every day.

For a nonprofit founder, getting uncomfortable means discarding the notion that you know everything in advance. It means taking the time to learn about the people you want to help (and their culture) first, and listen. And based on what you've dis-

covered, revising your approach in order to serve them effec-
tively—in a way that empowers *them.*

For a restaurant owner, getting uncomfortable means recognizing that your business involves much more than just food: It's
about every aspect of taste—branding, interior design, atmo-
sphere, social dynamics, trends, and culture. Being curious to
learn and perfect these skills or work with experts who might
challenge you to think beyond your initial assumptions.

For a shy creative, getting uncomfortable means learning to get
out of your shell—by finding out how to become a great com-
municator, and having the courage to self-promote.

. . .

These examples are just meant to make you think. Here, my
creative friend, I don't know what field you're a part of—but
you get the idea.

You must cultivate learning continuously throughout your life.
And always, always, always get uncomfortable. Think differently by learning skills outside of your field.

This is especially true if you're getting awards for the work
you're doing today!

Getting awards, money, comfort, or peer recognition means
you need to ask yourself:

"What's next?"

This is extremely important—and your answer must make

you feel slightly uncomfortable. If it doesn't, then you're not stretching yourself far enough.

Where do you need to grow? What's this thing you refuse to try that could make a huge difference? Creatively, for you, what's long overdue? What do you need to learn to market and self-promote yourself better? How are your presentation skills? Can you do public speaking?

● **Exercise: New Skills Challenge**
Write down three skills-related items that would make you uncomfortable (the ones you've been avoiding). Things you know could be a game-changer for you. Then, detail why these are important by explainning how they will impact your future:

Skill 1:

_____

Important because:

_____

Skill 2:

_____

Important because:

_____

Skill 3:

_____

Important because:

_____

I hope you'll grow your skills starting now and throughout your life. The greatness of your skills is directly proportionate to how uncomfortable you're willing to get. And in the Creative Dreaming Method, being uncomfortable is about confronting the Persona head on.

Growing continuously is what "having the right skills" means. Your skills must be always evolving. By trying new things that are outside of the scope of what you normally do, you will grow. You'll find new ideas.

Note: If you feel you're "too old" to start learning, or experiencing something new—watch out! This is another of Persona's tricks—don't fall for it. Take it from me: I learned how to drive at age 30. I left France and moved to the U.S. at 31. I relearned my entire software skill set and started practicing public speaking at 40. I pivoted my career at 44. I started being serious on social media at 47. It's never your age—it's your willingness to learn *and* grow. Your life is an ongoing adventure. If you're alive—you can do it!

Bonus Skill: Your Superpower
Yes, you have a superpower, and you probably don't know about it—because it comes so easily to you.

What's this unique thing you can do so well?

You think you know, right?

But do you, really?

● Exercise: The Superpower E-mail
Here, to find out what I'm talking about, you're going to ask

your friends/family. Don't skip this exercise; it can be life-changing. All it takes is sending five e-mails.

E-mail five of your friends, and simply ask:

"I'm reading this book on creativity called You Are a Dream, *and I'm answering a questionnaire. I would appreciate getting this answer from you.*

What do you think is my superpower (secret talent)? What is this one thing that I do so well in my life that I might not be aware of it?"

That's it.

Collect their responses and write down their answers:

According to my friends, my superpower is:

_____

_____

_____

_____

Now, take a look at what you've discovered, and ask yourself:

"Am I currently using my superpower to the fullest in my life? If not, what are three ways I could make that happen?"

_____

_____

_____

_____

My creative friend, as I just mentioned, this simple exercise can be life-changing. Therefore, if you think for a second, *"It's awkward to ask my friends this silly question,"* please tell your Persona to get over it and just do it.

Do you know your superpower? Are you using it every day in your life? These are powerful creative questions. And if you can answer "yes" every day, your life will be a wonderful, joyful adventure.

Your Point of View

After you've been perfecting your mindset (unstoppable) and your skills (ongoing, uncomfortable growth + using your super-power), something will happen—slowly but surely, you will develop a point of view.

A point of view is an original opinion you have about your field, the world, and your place in it.

A point of view is a long-term general direction in your thinking that you refine over the years.

In comparison, an insight is an instant breakthrough connected with a specific idea or project. It's your "Aha!" moment.

Your point of view is important—it always answers a set of questions that are connected with your taste or personal preference. To uncover it, simply look at something in your field, and ask yourself:

> *"Do I like this? Would I do it differently? How?"*

The opinion you have about what's happening in your field is directly connected with your capacity to be influential in it. To become a leader, you need to have an opinion, a vision of what's possible.

Having the right point of view means connecting your vision/opinion/taste with an audience, and expressing it authentically through your skills and message.

Challenge yourself to come up with ideas that are uncommon, ideas that express a real opinion you might have about taste, ethics, life, and people.

As a creator, you have ideas that are shaping how we see reality.

Here I'm going to give you an example. Imagine that you have a brand/activity/experience that talks to women.

What kind of image of a woman are you trying to portray? What's your point of view?

> Are you portraying:
> • an independent businesswoman (see DKNY in the 1980s)?
> • an office powerhouse (see J.Crew women)?
> • a glossy ultra-feminine goddess (see Tom Ford)?
> • a world-traveling bohemian (see Isabel Marant)?
> • a sporty, adventurous woman (see Patagonia)?
> • a decor-driven modernist (see *Dwell, Kinfolk*)?
> • an artist (see Comme des Garçons)?
> • an art curator (see Balenciaga)?
> • a craft artist/maker (see vintage OshKosh B'gosh)?

Choose wisely.

Choose wisely, because as you read this list, let's pretend that you're a fashion designer and your eyes start rolling with disdain. *"What kind of list is that! That's so limiting! I'm not interested in any of these portraits."*

Great—it means you have a real point of view.

What's your idea, then? Who is the woman that interests you?

You must be able to describe her, just as a novelist would his or her character.

How old is she? What does she do? Where does she live? What does she love/hate? What's the most important thing in her life? And so on.

Here, in our example, we're talking about the point of view you have for your audience, but the process is the same with a product, or an experience.

Let's take coffee.

Right now, in the United States, Starbucks is the leader in the coffee experience.

Now ask yourself honest questions:

"Do I like the Starbucks experience? Why? Or why not?"

_____

_____

_____

_____

"Is it relevant today?"

_____

_____

_____

_____

"Does it speak to me?"

_____

_____

_____

_____

"How would I do it differently?"

_____

_____

_____

_____

Please write down your answers, even if you have no intention of opening a coffee shop.

You get the idea. Your job as a creative is to develop your point of view and look out for insights—always, and everywhere. Develop your curiosity—ask yourself, *"How does it work?"* Read about subjects you know nothing about. Or ask people about their lives and what they're doing. Talk to them—it's enriching.

By using this approach, insights will come. And the more you research, the more you'll grow your point of view. With your point of view, you're painting a portrait of what reality, life, and people can be like. You're painting a picture of possibilities.

And if your point of view connects with the spirit of the times, you will succeed.

Your insight is your capacity to express your point of view for the right audience, at the right time, in the right way, using the right message.

. . .

Now let's focus on your point of view, in relationship to the field you're in. Let's go deeper.

Do you know the culture of your field? How so?

_____

_____

_____

_____

Who are the current top ten players in your field?

_____

_____

_____

_____

_____

_____

_____

_____

_____

_____

_____

_____

_____

Why are they leading?

_____

_____

_____

_____

_____

_____

_____

_____

Do you know the history of your field? Describe three breakthrough moments in the history of your field.

_____

_____

_____

_____

_____

_____

_____

_____

What was the most important breakthrough in your field?
Why?

_____

_____

_____

_____

_____

_____

_____

_____

_____

What could be the next breakthrough?

_____
_____
_____
_____
_____
_____
_____
_____

Do you know the history of the other fields that are related to your field? Which ones?

_____
_____
_____
_____
_____
_____
_____
_____

And there's more . . .

Do you know about art (low and high art), music, pop culture, films, TV, the Internet, youth culture, dance, sculpture, and craft—and how these could relate to your field? Write down three examples:

_____
_____
_____
_____
_____
_____

Do you currently have a unique point of view about your field?
Describe it:

_____

_____

_____

_____

_____

_____

_____

_____

_____

_____

_____

_____

Why is it unique? Will it connect with your audience? Why?

_____

_____

_____

_____

_____

_____

_____

_____

_____

_____

_____

_____

How can you create change in your field? Are you bringing an
evolution or a revolution?

_____

_____

_____

_____

_____

_____

_____

_____

_____

_____

_____

_____

The more you know about your field—your audience, life, and culture—the more you can refine your point of view.

Every creative project can be engaging, if the creators involved are honest. And honesty is always expressed by having a real opinion—an informed opinion based on accurate knowledge.

This point of view comes from understanding your field— knowing the culture you're a part of—and it often manifests itself as an insight, a flash of inspiration.

The insight is your personal truth. It is the foundation upon which your dream is built.

The insight is what's going to inform how you're going to direct your creative work and craft your message.

Bonus: The magical insight question: H.C.I.H.T.?
To get an insight (once you are entirely clear on who your audience is), simply ask yourself this powerful question, every single day: H.C.I.H.T.?

"How can I help them?"

The answer to this question, based on the simple idea of helping others, is what's going to make your creative project a success.

Why? Because if you can find a meaningful answer (your insight), you will make a difference in your audience's life. And once you make a difference, your audience will want to be engaged in what you have to offer. Therefore, you will be rewarded with creative success.

H.C.I.H.T. while working within an organization
"How can I help them?" works for a project that you create, but it can also have a tremendous effect in your career, if you work for an organization. In this context, when you ask, *"How can I help them?"* you're trying to identify how you can help your company. This will force you to think beyond your "job title" and come up with interesting creative ideas.

For example, when I was in my mid-twenties, I once worked within an organization that was trying to modernize their Web strategy. At the time, I was in charge of the art direction, the look and feel of the site. Yet, in the early meetings, I could see that the real problem with this project was not design, but the lack of understanding of marketing psychology: What were the core reasons why people would want to go on this site and interact with it?

So instead of thinking, *"I'm just going to do my job, and call it a day,"* I took the time to craft and share with the team a deeper strategic plan that offered a solution to the problem I had identified. And of course, to avoid bruising the egos of the mar-

keting people, I framed this plan under the "design category."
You might ask why I would do this extra work?

Because:

> • Even though at the time I received a salary, I treated
> my employer as my client (which is an empowering
> mindset). And as a golden rule: I'm here to help my
> clients succeed.
> • I want to work on projects that are successful. I'm
> going to do everything I can for this to happen. If the
> project is successful, it makes my life easier.
> • We are all in it together: If they win, I win.

And in this story, what ended up happening was that the site
became a huge success. The management recognized my
contribution, and I ended getting a massive raise. I was pro-
moted and my salary was doubled. Not bad for a few extra
hours of work.

H.C.I.H.T. with high-profile collaborations

A few years ago, I worked with the amazing electronic music
duo **Daft Punk**. At the time, I was creative director of an
independent art magazine, and I had figured out that creating
a special project with them would help us greatly (duh!). So I
decided to pitch them an idea.

Instead of thinking, *"Can I find a way to convince them to help
us?"* (i.e., what's in it for *me*), I simply asked myself, *"How can
I help them?"* (i.e., what's in it for *them*).

I discuss this thinking process in detail in my workshops, but
here I want you to imagine being in this position: You want to

do a feature with Daft Punk for your magazine. How can you help them?

And, to be clear, with high-profile collaborations, the answer is never: "Give them money," or "Promote them." Because on both counts they have more than their share already. You need to think on a deeper level. It's never these things that interest top creatives who are driven by their creative process. Your answer has to be meaningful.

Can you find a powerful idea?

And here, I would recommend that you bring in a classic acronym of the Creative Dreaming Method: W.A.I.T.T.

It means: **"Who am I talking to?"**

So, who are you taking to?

You're talking to Daft Punk.

Do you know their work?

You think so . . .?

How deeply?

It took me a full week to figure it out.

And the idea came because, despite the fact that I know them very well, I researched their work in depth. For a full week, I immersed myself in their entire body of work. I looked at everything. And the gem was hidden deep inside the research.

I found an insight about their work—something that no one had noticed before.

And so when I pitched them my idea, the project had value for them. Even though we were a small, independent magazine and they were this ultra-successful mega-band, I had found something that could benefit them. Something meaningful for them.

And that's why they said yes.

After we released the magazine, the project went viral online. It was a success, both for us and, more important, for *them*.

. . .

So, please remember, no matter where you are today, working on your project (or as part of a team inside of an organization)—and no matter how small you think you are—keep training yourself to find solutions. Keep asking:

> *"Who am I talking to?"*

> *"How can I help them?"*

Your Message

Now comes the last part of the Three Creative Assets: Designing the right message.

Your message, in a nutshell, is how you talk about yourself/ your work/your project to your audience.

The core of your message should be connected with your

insight. Your message should always be reflecting who you are and what you stand for.

This is important—your message should be honest and match your point of view and your actions. Today, a lot of brands make the mistake of crafting an inspiring message but offering an experience that directly contradicts it, so the audience ends up being horribly disappointed when it actually moves forward to interact with the brand.

Today, this lack of consistency is close to business suicide. Your message (or your brand's) must match the reality of what you're actually offering.

Next, the form of your message—how you're going to articulate it—should be based on your relationship with your audience. Here, the form is really important. You have to allow yourself to go outside of the expected norm. What really counts is your ability to connect.

For example, when Metro Trains in Melbourne, Australia, decided to create a message to prevent people from crossing the rails and getting into horrific accidents, they didn't go with the expected norms: gloomy pictures, statistics about deaths, or cameos by railway employees talking about the senseless loss of lives. Instead, they hacked the traditional format of an accident prevention campaign—by changing the form. They simply mocked the behavior they were trying to prevent with a catchy song—and an adorable animation called "Dumb Ways to Die." This video went viral on YouTube, getting more than 150 million views (as of 2017). Not bad for a prevention campaign.

Your message is important—spend some time on it. Revise it until you get it right.

● **Exercise: Your message.**

How are you unique? What do you stand for? Please write what your message is about by simply using a few keywords:

_____

_____

_____

_____

_____

_____

_____

_____

As an example, here's what my message is: creativity, growth, passion, and making a difference.

P.S. Are you curious about your message and building your brand? I wrote a little concept book on the subject: the aptly titled, *You Are a Message*. Feel free check it out.

THE THREE CREATIVE ASSETS ARE A RELATIONSHIP

One of the key concepts of this book comes from our Principle 5:

5. You are a relationship.

This simply means that everything in your life, including who you are, is an ongoing event interconnected with the Whole. In the same way, the Three Creative Assets are a relationship—they coexist as one.

Your mindset, your skills and point of view, and your message are working together.

One of the most effective ways to create change in your life is to alter one of them. Imagine that they are like the three end points of a triangle (vertices)—connected together. If you move one, it affects the shape of the whole.

Because your mindset, your skills and point of view, and your message exist through an organic relationship, they need to be driven by growth and change. Therefore, if you're serious about Creative Dreaming, it's important you refine these assets throughout your life. Change is good.

Refine. Refine. Refine. As a Creative Dreamer, you are walking on the path of mastery. You are building a work of art with your own life.

This is how you fill every day with joy: Look at it as an opportunity for growth. And the opportunity to grow for the rest of your life is one of the greatest gifts you have received from Life.

Use it.

. . .

And now, my creative friend, it's time to discover the Creative Dreaming Tactical Blueprint.

THE CREATIVE DREAMING TACTICAL BLUEPRINT

In the execution phase of the Creative Dreaming Method, we're going to use a specific Tactical Blueprint. This eight-step sequence demands real, honest work. Depending on the scope of your project, I suggest that you take at least ninety days (or more) to complete all the steps.

The sequence you'll discover here is inspired by the design thinking process—it can be used for any creative endeavor in life, art, or business. Design thinking was developed in the late 1960s and modeled after cybernetics. Today many top creative studios use it worldwide.

THE CREATIVE DREAMING TACTICAL BLUEPRINT

Part 1. Preparation
Step 1 – Be clear and specific about what you want to create.
Step 2 – Research; get the big picture.
Step 3 – Develop a point of view; imagine possibilities.

Part 2. Execution
Step 4 – Grow/Create.
Step 5 – Release, promote, and get feedback.

Part 3. Fine-Tuning & Expansion
Step 6 – Learn from feedback; fine-tune or revise.
Step 7 – Expand.
Step 8 – Repeat.

Note: The following is a condensed version of the process that takes place in my live events. It uses the same structure and methodology. Simply follow the steps and fill in the blanks.

PART 1. PREPARATION
Step 1 – Be clear and specific about what you want to create.

Most creatives have a hard time being clear and specific when they launch into a new project.

This may come from the faulty notion that if you're too specific you might lock yourself into something predictable.

That is not so with our process, because our goal is ongoing growth through feedback. Therefore, we're going to get as specific as possible.

So let's begin.

Q&A:

Today, what do you want to create?

_____

_____

_____

_____

If you're not sure because you have many ideas, pick the top three and write them here:

_____

_____

_____

_____

Now, please imagine we live in a strange dystopian future
where we must pay money to the government in order to be
able to work on our creative ideas. Out of these three ideas,
which one would you be willing to pay for because you couldn't
live without it?

_____

Great—we're going to select this idea first.

Now, remember, we've talked previously about your superpower. In what ways will your superpower help you realize this
idea?

_____

_____

_____

_____

Note: If there's a block here because you can't clearly see how
your superpower will be used for this idea, please try exploring
with a new idea. What we're trying to do here is find the right
match between your superpower and your creative idea.

For example: My superpower is my ability to digest and syn-
thesize complex ideas and communicate them to people in a
way that's inspiring. My dream has always been to become
a teacher. Today, this superpower (talking/communicating)
clearly supports the dream (teaching). It's really important that

you make this type of connection within your projects as well.

Are you ready to commit to this project long-term? Why?

_____

_____

_____

_____

Note: Here, we are looking for a long-term, meaningful dream versus a passing desire.

Ideally, what will happen if you commit to this for five years? How will you grow?

_____

_____

_____

_____

Ideally, what will happen if you commit to this for ten years? How will you grow?

_____

_____

_____

_____

Note: Creative Dreamers understand that life is change. By picturing yourself in the next ten years, you challenge yourself to have a long-term vision for your life. This is good. Every decade is an opportunity to grow: Your twenties, thirties, forties, fifties, sixties, seventies, eighties, and nineties . . . can all be a chance for growth. Don't worry if it's daunting to imagine yourself ten years from today—try it—see what comes up.

What's your audience for this project?

_____

_____

_____

_____

Note: If you've answered "everybody," you don't have an audience, because when you talk to everybody, you talk to no one. When it comes to your audience, it's very important to be as specific as possible. For example, if you write that your audience is "Youth: Aged 15–20," it is very vague. If instead you say: *"Rave kids who are into cosplay,"* you now have a clear picture of whom you're talking to. Knowing your audience is one of the most important parts of any creative project because it allows you to create a relevant message.

Can you start your project without breaking the bank? How are you going to finance it? Will it be sustainable?

_____

_____

_____

_____

Note: In Principle 8, we read, "Life sustains itself." It is important that you do the same. Financial sustainability is key. Saying, "I have six months to write my first music album, publish it, and sell it—and with the sales I'll be able to pay the rent" is not a good strategy. Instead, organize your life so that it supports your creative project financially. Start small by doing test runs, and slowly expand.

Step 2 – Research; get the big picture.

Research
We've already talked about your field and your audience before. This should be the core of your research.

You must answer these two questions for yourself through your research:

> – Who is my audience?
> – What are they looking for?

To get a real answer to these two questions, it's really important to encounter your audience in a meaningful way.

A lot of creatives make the mistake of saying, *"I know my audience because they are just like me."* This is not enough. You really need to listen. Get a feel for what's going on in the lives of your audience. What are they looking for? How can you help them make their lives better with what you do?

Example
While there are many ways to conduct research, I invite you to go out and talk to people. Conduct interviews. Spend time with them and write down what they actually say—in their own words (do not rephrase).

Your goal is to find the motivator behind their interest in your field. And here the work involves a bit of psychology. This is something that I discuss more during my live workshops, and it's beyond the space we have in this book. But I'd like to get you started. These are two great template questions you can ask your audience. Please adapt to your needs.

1. When it comes to _____ [your activity], why do you choose a specific brand/or person? How does it make you feel?

2. Once you have experienced/purchased it, how do your friends know about it? What does this tell them about you?

These two questions will reveal the true motivation of your audience. They will also give you insights on the possible direction of your project.

Get the big picture
Once you've spent enough time in your field, interacting with your audience, you will get the big picture by seeing how all the parts connect together. You will start to understand why certain trends occur in your field and why your audience makes specific decisions. This leads us to the next step . . .

Step 3 – Develop a point of view; imagine possibilities
Now that you understand your audience, it's time to develop your point of view.

Please describe your audience. Create two characters, describing them in detail. What do they want from life? What's their secret dream?

Character 1
Name: _____ Age: _____ Location: _____
Typical day: _____
Secretly wishes: _____

_____
_____
_____

Character 2

Name: _____ Age: _____ Location: _____

Typical day: _____

Secretly wishes: _____

_____
_____
_____

Now let's go back to you. Let's talk about your field . . . What's happening in your field right now?

_____
_____
_____
_____

Do you relate to the style, tone, and narrative of your field? Explain.

_____
_____
_____
_____

In your field, what doesn't work for you? What needs to be changed?

_____
_____
_____
_____
_____

How would you do it in a way that's meaningful for you?

_____

_____

_____

Imagine possibilities

Now that you have a point of view, imagine how your project
would look like, expressed in different ways.

For example, try imagining your project in different contexts.
Try different locations first. What would it be like for you to
work and live in San Francisco, New York, Los Angeles, Berlin,
or Paris? How about in a small town, connected to nature? Or
could your project be a part of nomadic adventure where you
travel throughout the year?

_____

_____

_____

_____

If your project is a product, can you create an experience?
If your project is an experience, can you create a product?

_____

_____

_____

_____

Would your project be better online, brick-and-mortar, or both?

_____

_____

_____

_____

A lot of these questions are meant to stimulate your imagination. If you're a beginner, they invite you to imagine what's not there yet and to consider many options. If you're already a working creative professional, these questions ask you to imagine what's next.

Today there's not just one way to be creatively successful. So think big. Try imagining as many scenarios and contexts as possible. By doing so, you will uncover pros and cons for every option. Let your imagination wander—try to get hold of the one that feels right for you at a gut level, then go for it.

Part 2. Execution
Step 4 – Grow/Create

Now it's time to start your project and grow/create. Here, I'm writing "grow/create" as one unit because in Creative Dreaming that's what you're looking for.

Creating will force you to confront numerous obstacles, in and out. You should be ready for them.

In the Creative Dreaming Method, by framing your project as a grow/create process you're essentially looking to learn and evolve by exposing yourself to reality and defining it as a process of growth.

Looking at your project like this—as a process—keeps you flexible by removing the pressure of a rigid outcome. It also keeps your mind open to the opportunities that will appear in front of you.

In addition, this grow/create mindset makes you flexible and unstoppable—and this is what you want.

We know that things will not always turn out the way you expect—and in the real world that's absolutely normal. For a Creative Dreamer, the grow/create mindset acknowledges it, and includes any obstacle as a part of your project.

Create
The act of creating must be integrated into your everyday life. It must become a habit.

All you need is about two hours per day to work on your project—regardless of what happens around you. You should be committed to this habit no matter what.

Here, if you think, *"I don't have time!"* Please reread Obstacle 6: Rational Excuses (page 180).

It's really important that you understand that your commitment must be iron-willed.

Resistance, procrastination, and blocks are all games of the Persona (see Part 1 and Part 2). For example, if you catch yourself procrastinating on social media rather than working on your project, instead of feeling bad about it, laugh it off. Say, *"Well played, Persona!"* and start working, even if you just have thirty minutes left. The more you do it, the more you'll get results.

Nothing should stop you from creating. And once you've made the decision to create, nothing will.

Little Bites

If you feel overwhelmed because your project seems too big (for example, writing a book), remember the "little bites" principle.

I once lived in a rental house in Los Angeles that had a termite problem. What I find fascinating about these small creatures is how the consistency of their little bites can create massive damage. I saw it firsthand when a large beam fell off from the house! (And it was time to find a better house.)

You, my creative friend, are bigger than a termite.

Every project that you can dream of can be chunked down into little bites.

It's really simple: You trace a timeline and write down the steps from beginning to completion. All you need to do is to complete one item in your timeline every day. If, every day, you keep going, you'll reach the finish line.

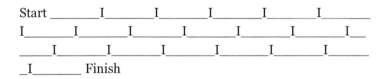

Example

When I write a book, my timeline looks like this:

> 1. Research and outline
> 2. Part 1
> 3. Part 2
> 4. Part 3

5. Part 4 (end of manuscript V1)
6. Manuscript revision V2
7. Manuscript revision V3
8. Copyediting
9. Art and design layout
10. First proof copy
11. Corrections and revisions
12. Second proof copy
13. Corrections and revisions
14. Third proof copy
15. Corrections and revisions
16. Finish

This process can take anywhere from six months to over a year and a half.

Then, after the book is completed, I create another timeline for sales and marketing.

No matter what your project is, it's really healthy for your process to work with a written timeline. In the Creative Dreaming Method, we act in order to grow. Once you have your timeline ready, you simply take a stab at each step, every day.

Ideally, you should post this timeline on your wall—say, next to your desk or work area.

If one day you skip your work, come up with a block, etc., write it down in your Persona Awareness Journal—and immediately go back to work.

Your Persona doesn't like things out in the clear (awareness), and much prefers to direct you into the when-I-feel-like-it-zone (unawareness). Don't fall for it.

Get super-clear. Get it done. Move to the next step.

Remember, in the Creative Dreaming Method, your focus is on your process.

Step 5 – Release, promote, and get feedback
Release and promote
In order to release your project properly, you'll also need to figure out a promotion strategy.

This is extremely important. While there are a million ways to do promotion and marketing, I'm just going to talk about the most effective and cost-effective one (it's free): getting people excited about what you do. This is what professionals call word-of-mouth marketing.

Because we live in an interconnected world, your goal is to invite your first users to actively promote what you do. And if you deliver something special, they should be happy to do so—if they are engaged with what you do. And it's your job as a creator to figure out how to create this link.

Here, I'd like to continue using the example of my books. My previous titles *You Are a Circle* and *You Are a Message* are entirely self-published. These books truly are a phenomenon—I'm always surprised, for example, when I have a single retail store ordering one hundred copies and then reordering just three months later! It's simply amazing.

And when it comes to promoting the books, my readers are my ambassadors. They love the books and talk about them. They buy copies for their friends. They post about them on social media. I'm very lucky.

But is it just luck? Yes and no.

In my books I have a page where I tell my readers that these books are part of a self-publishing experiment (because they are). Then, I simply ask them to join in and be "part of the team," so to speak, by posting about the books. And, because my readers are awesome, they do it.

By the way, if you like this book and want to share it on your favorite social media platform, please do so and use the hashtag **#YouAreADreamBook**. You can also tag me on Instagram **@profg.co** . . . Thank you! I appreciate your support.

Note 1. Here, I really want to be as honest as possible. Creating this special connection with your audience is not easy. It takes time, and it also takes the right audience. Today, I'm lucky to have an amazing audience—they get it. They support the project.

So before you release your project please make sure that your promotional strategy is part of the project itself.

The way to look at this is to think about your creative project as a way to build a community.

Note 2. A lot of creative people look down on marketing, thinking it's below them and their creative practice. This is a mistake because it's critical to understand that—as a creator—you are your best promoter. If you know nothing about marketing, you should learn about it and find a way to apply it in your project by experimenting; see what works. Marketing is also something that we look at in detail in my live workshops because your creative project is never finished unless it includes a successful marketing strategy.

More on word of mouth, and authenticity

Using word of mouth as a promotion strategy can take many shapes and forms. It really doesn't matter what category you're in:

You must create (and facilitate) a space for your audience to talk about what you do.

In fashion, this could be creating a brand that only the "initiates" know about. Because (and this is something I constantly tell my students), *"fashion is initiation."* For example, the shoe brand Common Projects (check them out) chose to avoid putting a logo on their sneakers; instead, they decided to print a ten-digit number unique to each shoe design. The result? Instant curiosity and conversations. *"What are these shoes? Who made them?"*

You can apply this strategy in any field.

For example, in the business of food and restaurants this initiation process is the same. A chef will start a concept, and at first, just the cognoscenti know about it. And if the experience is unique, they will spread the word.

The reason why this approach works is because—today—your audience is looking to discover something authentic. And as a creative, from your perspective, the way to deliver an authentic experience is to focus on your process, in such a way that it will start conversations. It's important to ask yourself how your audience is going to discover your work (in what context), and how authentic your offer/product/experience will feel to them.

For example, my three books for the "You Are" series (*You Are a Circle, You Are a Message*, and *You Are a Dream*) all include woodblock print illustrations. My process was to cut each woodblock by hand and then apply ink with a roller to create a unique print. While this process is very time consuming, it's authentic. I truly enjoy creating visuals this way.

When a reader (a creative) discovers the book for the first time in a cool hipster store, he/she knows—just by holding it—that this is the real deal. Next, when a friend goes to the reader's house and sees one of these books, the same thing happens again. By seeing the handmade feel of the book, the readers know it comes from an authentic place.

And this trend goes beyond publishing—it's taking place in every category. This is a great opportunity for creatives to bring something authentic, new and refreshing.

Globally, there's a search for authenticity. This opens possibilities for independent artists—or even entirely new markets—to emerge.

Be authentic. By expressing your truth you are connecting with your True Self.

In addition, this approach will also position you in the minds of your audience as a trusted source they want to interact with. It will make them want to talk about and share what you do with others.

How can you create curiosity and conversations with
your project?

_____

_____

_____

_____

In what ways is your project authentic? How does your process
reflect this authenticity?

_____

_____

_____

_____

Partnering with others

In the Creative Dreaming Method, we always look at life as an
interconnected Whole. This means that as a creative, you are
not isolated. Many beginner creatives think that they are com-
peting against one another. This is a critical mistake. And this
mistake is, of course, a Persona-driven idea that comes from a
sense of lack. In reality you are *not* surrounded by competitors,
but by peers.

This is easy to understand. Whatever category you're in, you
are sharing the same audience with your peers. This audience
is not captive: Sometimes they will interact with you; sometimes they will interact with others.

If you apply the Creative Dreaming Method with focus, you
will develop a unique voice in your field. As you do so, you will
also notice other players that share the same work ethic as

you, each with a unique voice as well. When this happens, it's a smart idea to connect with them and offer to support them.

That's right. Support *them* first.

Once this supportive relationship is established, you can talk shop and freely exchange ideas that will make you both grow. This is how partnerships are formed.

When you partner with others, you are stronger. You can share promotion strategies and ideas. Or you can even cross-promote, meaning that you can include them in your promotional efforts, while they include you in theirs.

Today, big companies often use this strategy. That's why you see, for example, brands like Apple partnering with Hermès, Ford with Harley-Davidson, NikeLab with Marc Newson, etc. Each partnership works to the advantage of both parties.

And all the smart creatives are doing it, too. In music it's a common practice. For example, the electronic duo Daft Punk collaborated with Kanye West, Pharrell Williams, The Weeknd, etc., while Pharrell has also collaborated with The Weeknd, and more surprisingly with the contemporary artist Takashi Murakami (among many others). The higher you rise as a creative, the more likely it is that you will collaborate with your peers.

There is a really simple reason for it. A creative kinship exists in the world, and when you recognize it in others, they'll recognize it in you as well.

When, a few years ago, I was interviewing top creatives about their work process, they all agreed on that point:

Collaborations and support are key. My partner-in-crime, magazine editor-in-chief Katy Donoghue, conducted an interview with Pharrell Williams that drove this point home perfectly. He said:

> *"You know your people when you meet them . . . It's a thing we all have where we don't see limits, limits are just mild challenges, and we'll do anything to help something manifest into existence. I admire that in other people so much"* (*Whitewall* Magazine, Issue 16).

So, my creative friend, start interacting with your peers, collaborate, and cross-promote. You'll be more successful for it.

Timing
One of the most important aspects of releasing a project is to find the right timing for it. For example, please be aware of major holidays, or anytime your audience is taking a break from their regular life. You need to figure out when and where is the best time to connect with your audience—and it really depends on the nature of your project.

Conversely, there are also great moment and places in the calendar when your audience comes together as one, such as venues, conferences, trade shows, or festivals. A date like one of these could be the perfect timing for launching your project. Again, learning about the culture of your field will point you in the right direction.

Part 3. Fine-Tuning & Expansion
Step 6 – Learn from feedback; fine-tune or revise

You've just launched your project, and now you see if it's working or not: This is your feedback. If it's not working, go back to the drawing board and tweak it. Then repeat until you get it right.

Feedback can be brutal, yes. But remember, this is also an opportunity to learn. In fact, without feedback, you have nothing. Because your project is a creative experiment and a process, get the feedback and use it as an opportunity to do better.

Growing through your feedback is the foundation for Creative Dreaming—and negative feedback is often a hidden invitation to reach outside of your comfort zone. No matter what, embrace your feedback—use it to learn, grow, and improve.

Steps 7 & 8 – Expand and Repeat.
Now that you have created this feedback loop between your audience and your project, it's time to ask this great question:

> *"What's next?"*

Creative Dreaming is a lifelong activity that will keep your mind forever young and growing. "What's next?" allows you to take a deep breath, look back at your accomplishments, and start dreaming again. Expand what you have already created or create a new dream.

Go back to Step 1. Repeat!

That's it; these are the eight steps. As you can see, this approach is focused on getting results through the relationship between you, your project, and your audience. The Creative Dreaming Method always acknowledges the Whole. And interacting successfully with this Whole demands integration.

INTEGRATION: THE SECRET TO BECOMING AN UNSTOPPABLE CREATIVE FORCE

Now, one idea I'm inviting you to keep thinking about is integration.

Are all the parts related to your creative life fully integrated? Is everything and everyone in your life aligned with your creative project or dream?

Or are these parts fragmented and going in different directions?

Integration is the secret to becoming an unstoppable creative force. When all the important moving parts (situations and people) are working in the same direction, creative success is simply a matter of time.

Here, I'm going to share with you a checklist that will help you to quickly assess where you are today.

Look at these elements. See if they align with your goal. Circle Yes or No. If No, write down what you can do to bring them in alignment.

CREATIVE PROJECT CHECKLIST

Your Creative Project is _____

_____

Creation: conception + execution

Do you have the skills involved to conceptualize and execute
your project? (Yes/No)

This can be improved by _____

_____

_____

_____

_____

_____

Culture of your field

Do you know the culture of the field you're entering in depth
(the history, players, trends, and countertrends)? (Yes/No)
Do you know the audience you're talking to? (Yes/No)
Do you know the field so well that you have developed an original point of view (are you offering something unique)? (Yes/No)

This can be improved by _____

_____

_____

_____

_____

_____

Branding

Can you create a brand (or personal brand) that is relatable for your specific audience? (Yes/No)

Does your brand have a lifestyle component? (Yes/No)

This can be improved by _____

_____

_____

_____

_____

Marketing/Storytelling

Is your launch strategy ready? (online/offline)? (Yes/No)

Have you created a meaningful, powerful, and engaging story to promote your project? (Yes/No)

Have you selected your launch platforms? (Yes/No)

This can be improved by _____

_____

_____

_____

_____

People

Are you surrounded by people who support you? (Yes/No)

Do you get inspiration from your closest friends? (Yes/No)

This can be improved by _____

_____

_____

_____

_____

YOUR FIRST STEP, AND THE SIX DOMAINS OF LIFE
Now, my creative friend, you might have a very important question:

> *"Where should I start?"*

Well, it depends . . . If you say, "I really want to write a story and publish it," then simply get to work on this project. But as you've probably imagined, the Method is not limited to artistic projects. It can be applied to any area of life.

In the Creative Dreaming Method workshops, we specifically look at six aspects of your life.

The Six Domains of Life
1. Self-expression/Exploration
2. Work and Finance
3. Health/Mind-Body
4. Relationships
5. Art of Living
6. Purpose/Spiritual Life

These Six Domains are a living relationship, and this relationship forms who you are today.

As you now understand, the Creative Dreaming Method is a way to put intent in your reality in order to alter it positively— by bringing joyful growth. Once this becomes a habit you can apply it to any domain.

Because everything is interconnected (see Principle 3 and Principle 4), every gesture you take affects the whole. And this is where it gets really exciting.

In *You Are a Dream*, we've talked a lot about starting a creative practice. Here, as an example, I'll pick sculpture.

Sculpture is not isolated. As with any creative pursuit, it's a part of multiple domains, such as:

> **1. Self-expression/Exploration:** With sculpture, I'm being self-expressive and I push myself outside of my comfort zone.

> **2. Work and Finance:** Because there are costs associated with sculpture, I need to organize my finances really well. I also need to start a marketing plan to promote my work if I want to sell it.

> **3. Health/Mind-Body:** My work as a sculptor is a way to pacify my busy mind. The more I create, the more I grow. Because sculpture is very physical and involves heavy materials, the work demands that I'm in the best shape I can be. I work out and eat healthy food to be strong.

> **4. Relationships:** My sculpture work is an opportunity to see how viewers interact with my pieces. Each piece affects people differently. I also have conversations about life with peers that connect with my work.

> **5. Art of Living:** In order to sculpt, I have adapted my life in such a way that it sustains my practice. To thrive, I've embraced my community by having open studio days and giving lectures and workshops. My art has become my art of living.

6. Purpose/Spiritual Life: I've decided to use my art to make a difference. My work helps raise funds for nonprofits I've partnered with. And, when I'm alone with my work, I sometimes experience a moment of quiet grace. At a deeper level, my work connects me with the transcendent.

As you can see, everything is always interconnected. So, again, let's go back to your question:

"Where should I start?"

Here's the incredibly good news: You can start wherever you want. In the Creative Dreaming Method, we're not just about reaching a goal, but growing through a process.

You can pick any domain from the list, because when you use the Method correctly, it will affect every other domain.

If, for example, you pick Health/Mind-Body and focus on it, it will affect your five other domains automatically. As long as you bring full awareness and creativity into your actions, the results will touch every aspect of your life.

And there's one more thing . . . Once you've been practicing the method for a while, you can take a closer look at the domains in your life and discover the relationships that connect them. And as you do, you can start working on the Six Domains simultaneously. This is where your life becomes a path based on integration—every aspect supporting the Whole.

This is the path of mastery. And supporting this integration throughout your life is both the path and the reward.

● **Exercise: The Six Domains of Life**

Think about your dream, or creative project, and write down how it will contribute to your growth and well-being in the Six Domains of your life.

As you do this exercise, get clear on the idea that all these aspects are interconnected. Whatever activity you choose to pursue, the more integrated it is, the more likely you will succeed.

How my project is going to contribute to my:

1. Self-expression/Exploration

_____
_____
_____
_____
_____
_____

2. Work and Finance

_____
_____
_____
_____
_____
_____

3. Health/Mind-Body

_____
_____
_____
_____
_____
_____

4. Relationships

_____

_____

_____

_____

_____

_____

5. Art of Living

_____

_____

_____

_____

_____

6. Purpose/Spiritual Life

_____

_____

_____

_____

_____

_____

Note: As you will find out, creative life demands total commitment and total integration. All the moving parts must move in unison. At first, it might seem a daunting, impossible task—and that's okay. Take your time. Remember, **as a Creative Dreamer, your goal is to fine-tune your approach throughout your life.**

RITUAL OF POWER

In our conversation together, I've challenged you to think about your life in a new way. I've shared with you a map that connects your creativity and growth into a dynamic Whole. I've also presented you with a blueprint, an action plan to get you started.

And now it's time to talk about one big item:

Time.

Remember, in the Creative Dreaming Method, we focus on the creative process itself; not the image of a rigid outcome we think we want. We allow ourselves to be open to the process. This perspective, or shift, allows for discoveries and insights to occur, leading to the inner growth that will bring the realization of our dream. In other words, the dream comes into reality when we focus on the process itself (ongoing and proactive), not from "wanting it now" (the Persona's entitlement).

Once you have integrated this shift into your life, things will start changing, and often in ways that are more meaningful than originally imagined.

This is the gift of the Method.

But, in the beginning, there's an adjustment period that needs to take place. We have to break through our limited perception of time.

You see, in our society, we have been taught since childhood to value speed over depth.

From overnight success stories and instant celebrity to get-rich-quick opportunities, mainstream culture keeps telling us that faster is always better, that cutting corners is the way to go. It's *not*.

This notion explains why, in Western societies, we live in financial abundance, yet, paradoxically, we experience the everyday as an anxiety-inducing "rat race," where enough is never enough. And this frenzy for speed has now caught up with the rest of the planet as well.

Just like an addiction, it never fulfills us; instead, it keeps us wanting more:

> We want a speedy (and predictable) outcome.
> Then, a new one.
> Then, another one.

This thirst for speedy results is a Persona game being played on a large scale. By displacing our focus on outside results, it denies the possibility of any meaningful change inside.

Creative Dreamers know that this approach is broken because:

Depth—not speed—is where it's at.

In your own creative life, this means that you need to get ready to confront your own addiction to speed, first, in order to uncover the gem of depth.

How is it done, concretely? How do you keep working, and growing for years, without seeing apparent results?

How do you keep your focus long-term, if there are no immediate rewards? Because, you see, I know very well that when I'm saying, *"The process itself is its own reward,"* this can be really hard to get when you're starting out. You might think, *"Are you kidding me?"*

I've been there, believe me. Being naturally impatient, I have found handling delayed results to be one of the most excruciating challenges to tackle.

Because it doesn't matter if, intellectually, you get the idea or if you've reread this book a hundred times. Time delays can bend the strongest resolve.

Time is the ultimate teacher: it will test your creative willpower, your enthusiasm, your commitment.

So now I'd like to share with you a way to stay focused long-term, by introducing a technique that will bypass the Persona's nagging (*"There are no results yet! You're wasting your time!"*). This age-old practice is common to many ancient cultures and it brings its own rewards.

This technique is called rituals.

A ritual is a symbolic action (completed with full awareness) that has a special meaning for you.

Traditionally, a ritual is often associated with a prayer or a rite of passage. But with deep intent, a simple, everyday practice can become a ritual: making tea, arranging flowers, preparing food, walking in nature, gardening, or playing a musical instrument.

It's not so much what your ritual is that counts; it's how much awareness you put into it and the meaning you attach to it. It's how much you infuse it with your soul.

In the Creative Method, because we're joy-based, we're using rituals in a unique way—as a soulful thank you for working on your creative process.

It's very simple: You pick something that you love or that's important for you, and you connect it symbolically with your creative work.

For example, I love the smell of burning incense (Japanese incense is the best). It's my personal ritual.

This is how I use my ritual when I work. I break down what I need to do for the week into ten items. I have a simple bowl filled with sand where I've placed ten incense sticks. Every time I complete an item on my list, I burn one stick. The gesture and the smell create a pleasant mood that tells me (symbolically): *"Congratulations. You're moving in the right direction."*

And therefore, thanks to this practice (which has been in my life for over three decades), I've become extremely patient—to the point where I can delay gratification indefinitely—because the process itself is enjoyable.

Here, there's a very important point:

In the Method, the symbolic gesture (the reward of the ritual) comes *after* the completion of a certain task (I don't burn incense before I start working).

And if, for whatever reason, I slack off: There's no incense. Period. And when I do slack off . . . something happens. Because I'm so attached to my simple ritual, after a day or two, I will always go back to work and do what needs to be done.

The ritual is powerful because it's both very personal, and meaningful. It's an unbreakable agreement that you make with your True Self. It's a way to honor your creative spirit. With your gesture, you acknowledge it. You thank it. And, in a way, because there's an exchange taking place through the ritual, your True Self thanks you back.

A ritual is a symbolic gesture that connects the present moment with the Whole. It reminds you that—no matter how mundane or challenging your day is—you are connected with everything else. It reminds you that what you do matters.

I invite you to experiment with this practice in your own life. Introduce a simple ritual that acknowledges that, through your creative work, you are celebrating your True Self. When you do, you'll be able to handle any delays and setbacks because the ongoing ritual will reinforce that the fact that you are progressing.

Note: As I am writing this, I'm noticing that it's 7:23 p.m. I've been writing all day and I've completed my work.

Now, guess what?

It's time to burn an incense stick!

YOUR THREE LEVELS OF DREAMING

My creative friend, we're about to end our time together. And before we say goodbye, I'd like to share one last important aspect of the Creative Dreaming Method.

It's about integrating your Creative Dreaming practice so it fulfills you throughout your life. We call it the **Three Levels of Dreaming**. It's a three-point list that sounds a little bit like a poem. It goes like this:

> **Dream for Now,**
> **Dream for Tomorrow,**
> **Dream for Life.**

And now, I'd like to invite you to think about Creative Dreaming in three levels of time simultaneously. This practice is perhaps the most important in the Method, and that's why I have kept it for the end.

Dream for Now

Here, you start with what you want today. This dream is more akin to a goal: It could be something really simple, fun, or material. It's also the one that requires the least inner change. You can select three to five items that you'd love to see in your life—like a wish list.

You could say: I want a new studio, a super-clean house, a new job, a vacation, etc.

In order to realize this Dream for Now—you will need to focus and experiment—working diligently toward this goal by using our blueprint.

Dream for Tomorrow

Here, you are going deeper. You're imagining your future five to ten years from now. How would you like to evolve in the coming years? What qualities would you like to cultivate? Ideally, how would you be living your life in five or ten years?

Dream for Tomorrow is about inner change through growth. Pick the areas of your life where you could do better: Who would you become, if you moved beyond these limitations? What would your life be like?

Starting from where you are today, take the time to imagine how you can evolve into the best "you" you can be. Dream for Tomorrow is about making meaningful changes that will have a long-term impact: Studying, starting a new career or business, learning new skills, cultivating new relationships, creating new health habits, bringing more authenticity in your life.

Here, it's an opportunity to get a clear view of the power of long-term commitment. You picture yourself dedicating five to ten years to one specific dream and see how you will be changed by the process.

Dream for Life

This is a space in which to think about your life at a higher level. Ask yourself:

> *"How can I make a difference through my life?*
> *What legacy will I leave behind?"*

Dream for Life by aligning your dreams, goals, and aspirations so they feed your soul. Recognize that your life is a spiritual adventure.

By acknowledging that your life is a finite experience, you can look at it as a way to contribute to the Whole. Here, the shift is from "Me" to "We."

. . .

The Three Levels of Dreaming is a way to make decisions about your own life by playing with the structure of time and with scale. This approach is called trinary thinking; it means that you simultaneously hold three ideas (that seem to be unrelated); and you play with them until the resulting whole becomes harmonious.

The practice of trinary thinking is one of the easiest modules to understand, but it's one of the most challenging.

Why?

Because it's extremely hard for us humans to think about our own future, especially a future where we'll become a different person (and we all will be different in the future, whether we like it or not!). It's hard, simply because the Persona panics when we strategize about change and growth.

And so here, the Three Levels of Dreaming is my final challenge for you. Or more accurately, this is my final challenge for your Persona—and its voracious resolve to keep you the same.

Take a deep breath. Connect with your True Self, and look at your life as an open space of possibilities.

See yourself grow and evolve in five to ten years. Connect the person you are today with your future self. Remember, everything is interconnected—and so are your past, present, and future selves. The doors leading to growth are open.

Who will you become?

Imagine yourself evolving in the direction of your dreams. Imagine yourself being more creative, more loving, more passionate, more engaged, more connected, more strategic, more adventurous . . .

Take the time to really visualize this. Ask yourself:

>   *"How will I grow?"*

Because you see, my creative friend, your evolution through time is the key to all your dreams.

● **Exercise: Your Three Levels of Dreaming**
Please take a moment to think about the big picture. Imagine how your dreams can fulfill you throughout your life.

Write down your Three Levels of Dreaming:

My Dream for Now

_____
_____
_____
_____
_____
_____
_____
_____

_____
_____
_____

My Dream for Tomorrow

_____
_____
_____
_____
_____
_____
_____
_____
_____
_____

My Dream for Life

_____
_____
_____
_____
_____
_____
_____
_____
_____
_____
_____
_____
_____

CONCLUSION

My creative friend, we have now reached the end of the book. Congratulations!

Together, we've been through a complete process. In our conversation, we have been looking at Creative Dreaming as a tool for transformation and growth. A process that can transform your own life, a way of creative living that can make a positive impact in the world.

Here, before we say goodbye, I'd like to invite you to reflect a little bit more on our Principle 4:

4. Every complex living system only exists in relationship to the Whole.

This principle means that your dream is connected with every aspect of the reality you live in. Every time you start a creative project (no matter how small you think it might be), you're changing your reality. Or more accurately, you're changing your reality/self.

There's another implication for this that's very exciting:
Every time you create a new dream, it affects not only every aspect of your life—it also affects us all.

Therefore, in this journey, remember that you are not alone.

You matter.
Your adventure is our adventure.
Because we are all connected.
Because we are all in this dream *together*.

You can dream bigger dreams. You can dream with certainty. You can imagine what's not there yet, and make it real.

Think about it.

Life has given you an amazing gift.

> Feel it.
> Honor it.
> Nurture it.

Use it, starting today—and for the rest of your life.

Because now, the real work begins.

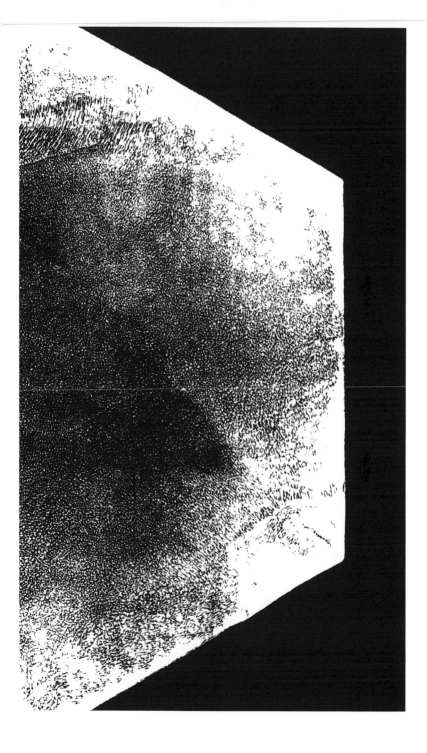

Always adapt to the new. Stay open to the possibilities that are right in front of you.

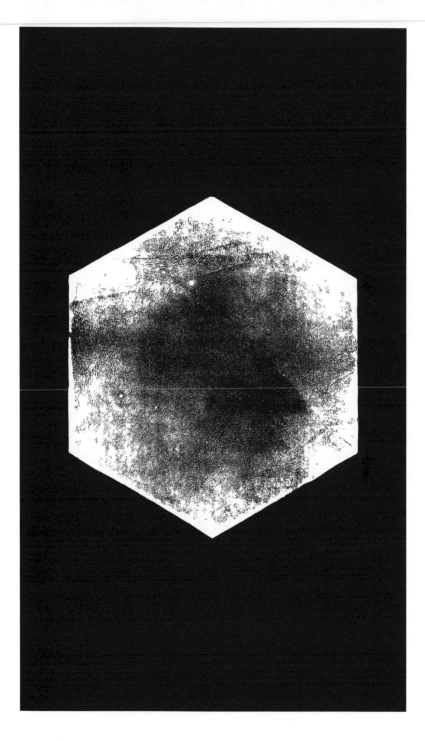

Keep asking:
"Who am I talking to?"
"How can I help them?"

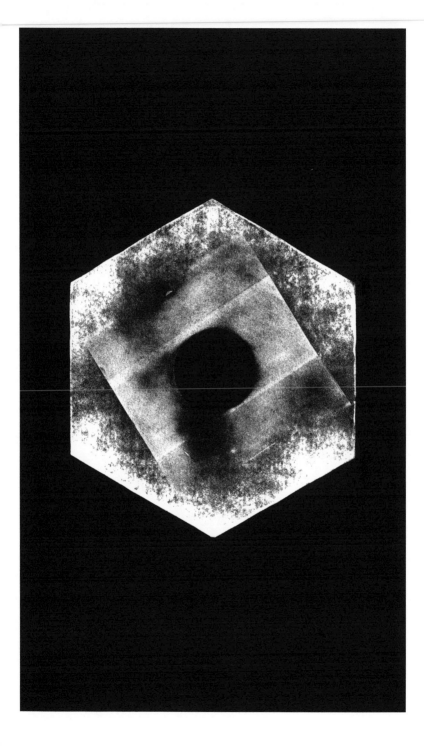

Refine. Refine. Refine. As a Creative Dreamer, you are walking on the path of mastery. You are building a work of art with your own life.

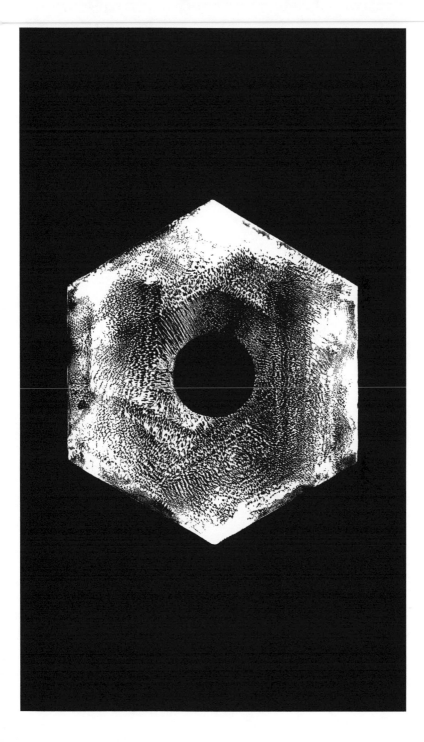

Be authentic. By expressing your truth
you are connecting with your True Self.

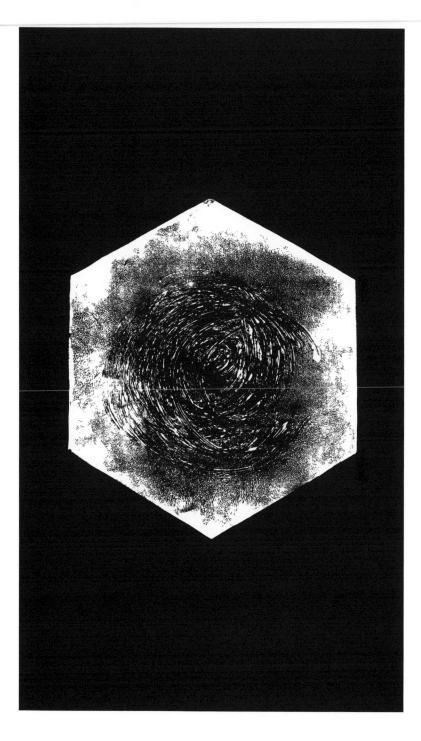

Depth—not speed—is where it's at.

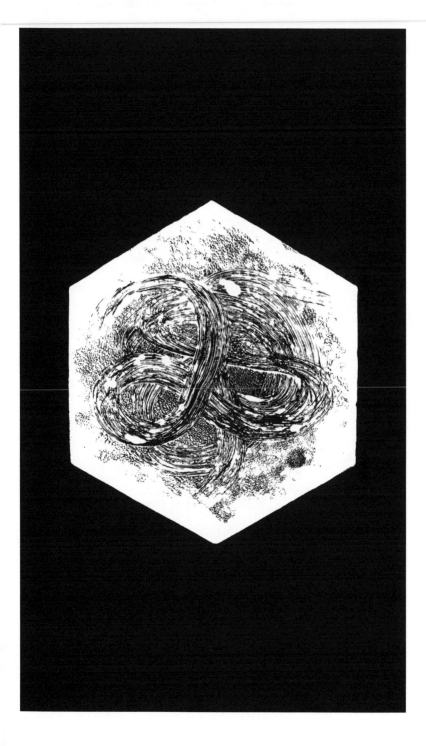

Dream for Now,
Dream for Tomorrow,
Dream for Life.

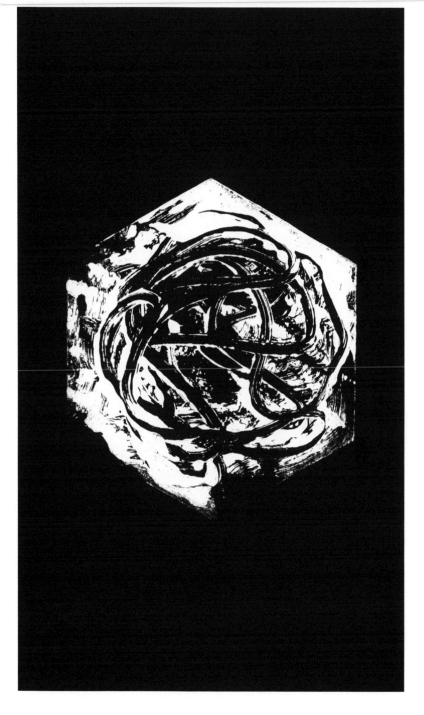

You matter.
Your adventure is our adventure.
Because we are all connected.
Because we are all in this dream *together*.

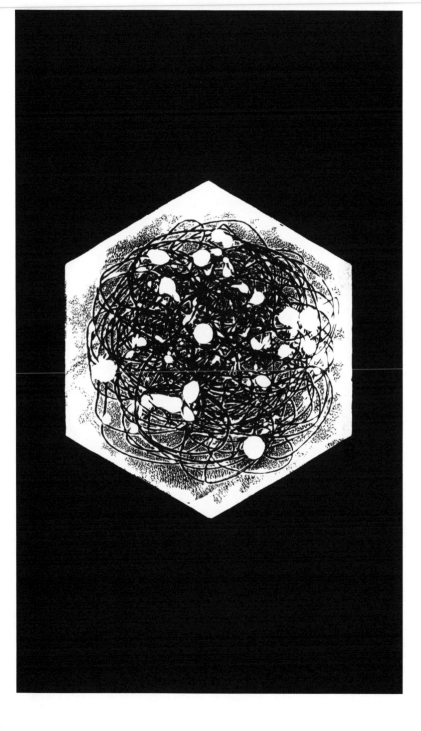

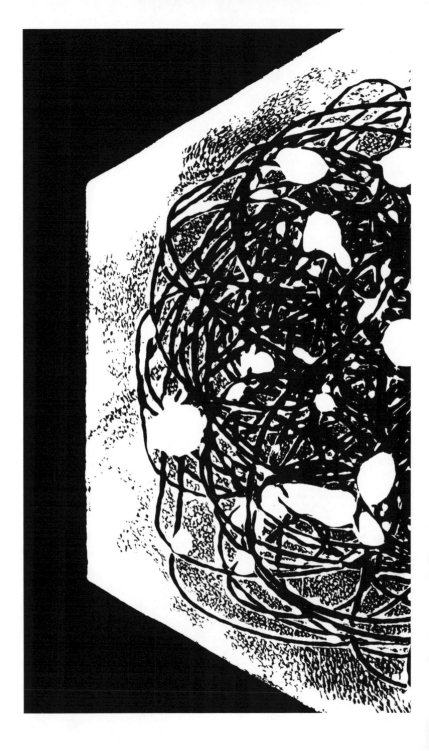

LATE

NIGHT

TALK

Guillaume Wolf "Prof. G" talks with Joanne Abellera about some of the ideas presented in *You Are a Dream*.

Fiber artist and fashion designer Joanne Abellera is Guillaume Wolf's life partner. Together, they live and work in their mountain home in Lake Arrowhead, California, with their daughter.

This conversation took place late in the night.

LIFE AS A CREATIVE PRACTICE

JA: *In the book, you write about practicing awareness. Can you explain the connection with creativity?*

GW: In the map I present in the book, I offer that the creative act is inherently connected with Life itself. Meaning that if you're alive Life's creative force runs through you, no matter what. Even if you refuse to acknowledge it, it's there. And once you become conscious of this process—by practicing awareness—you're able to create a space for your creativity and growth to unfold. Creative Dreaming is about using awareness through the creative gesture. This is the key to transformation and change.

JA: *But not everyone is an artist, right?*

GW: Of course not, not in the common sense. However, everyone can be an artist of the present moment . . . You can be an artist of your own life, today.

JA: *You wrote, "Your life is, and has always been, a creative practice."*

GW: That's right. And when awareness is there, it really doesn't matter who you are: You can be a gardener, a mechanic, a contractor, a mom, a teacher, a librarian, an entrepreneur, a student, an artisan, a chef, or a nurse . . . Your "title" is completely irrelevant. If you put awareness into what you do, you'll find out that the greatest adventure you can dream of is your very own life—starting where you are today. It's this journey of growth that each one of us is called to realize. Letting go of the role you're playing and finding the treasure that's within, finding "the you that's you."

This is a very powerful realization. It's right here! [*Snaps his fingers*] It's right now! [*Snaps his fingers*]

JA: *But awareness has to be there, right?*

GW: Yes. But to be clear, even if you don't practice awareness, the creative process will still unfold anyway. But this time it will be driven by your Persona, not your True Self. However, if you bring awareness into your own life, you give your True Self a chance to arise.

THE TRUE SELF

JA: *You mention the True Self in the book, but you don't expand on it very much . . . Why?*

GW: Yes, this is because you have to experience it for yourself. You can get in contact with it through the creative act.

The True Self is the true "you." For example, it's this part that you can feel when you experience awe.

JA: *But a lot of famous artists are also known to be horrible egocentrics—driven entirely by their Persona. Isn't it a contradiction?*

GW: No. It's because the people you're referring to simply got burned by the fame/power game—which is the curse of the successful artist and another trick of the Persona. The origin of the authentic creative gesture is always the True Self, and if fame or power comes into play later, it's a perfect angle for the Persona to regain control by saying, *"Look! You're a genius! You're better than the rest!"* Which is terrible, because if you believe it, your creative life is instantly over. You become stuck in this unattainable image—you stop growing—and you'll live in constant pain just to maintain this illusion. This is why you see great artists suddenly drying out. Overnight, they turn into has-beens. It's because they have fallen for that Persona trap. And when this happens, regardless of the amount of fame or money they have accumulated, their lives become a living hell. It's not a pretty picture.

But what we're talking about here has nothing to do with the thirst for fame or power. It's not what the Method is about.

JA: *I agree.*

GW: What we're talking about is this: There is a mystery connected with the creative gesture. It's deeply transformative both personally and collectively. Anyone can experience it. When you experiment with Creative Dreaming—by bringing awareness in your life through a creative act—you allow your

True Self to unfold. And when this happens, you see how magical, beautiful, and meaningful Life can be.

JA: *But what is this True Self?*

GW: It's the part of you that recognizes that you and I are not separate . . . The True Self is a whole in relation with the Whole. The True Self is an intimate experience that's meant to be lived. It unfolds as part of a transformation process linked with Creative Dreaming. It arises when you're courageous enough to start your creative journey with complete honesty by facing the hurdles and growing from the experience.

DEPTH CREATIVITY

JA: You Are a Dream *seems to live within its own universe, and yet you touch upon many different fields. What category are you in? Is it Creativity? Psychology? Spirituality?*

GW: Well . . . For someone who sees everything as being inter-connected, this is a trick question!

JA: *Is it? For example, in the book you mention the creation of the Persona. Isn't it psychology?*

GW: Well . . . not quite.

JA: *What's the difference?*

GW: First, what I describe here is not meant to be used as a healing practice or a substitute for therapy. It is very important to be clear on that.

So the work presented in this book is a process of self-discovery for the healthy, creative mind. I'm using a map to help us think about Life, one that starts with the fact that everything is interconnected, then goes on by offering that Life is driven by a creative process, including the creation of a fake, conditioned "self"—which we call the Persona—that's in direct contrast with the True Self. These axioms, and the methods that follow them are not the territory of psychology. In a way, they are more related to certain views present in Zen Buddhism or some Western esoteric traditions.

I'm interested in exploring the creative process in depth. And the conceptual map I'm using is applied to explore uncharted territories—such as transcendent states of being, self-discovery, personal growth, and the creative insight.

JA: *Transpersonal states have traditionally been explored through philosophy or religion . . . You've just mentioned Zen.*

GW: Yes, and while I love spiritual philosophy and religion, both are deeply entrenched in cultural biases and dogmas —which happen to be known killers of the creative process. Zen, for example, is an incredibly radical practice that's rooted in Japanese culture. And a culture-heavy tradition is always self-contained—because it *has* to be. You cannot "adapt it" without altering its very essence. Therefore, an ancient tradition is never a place for ongoing innovation, exploration, and new ideas. Otherwise, it would simply cease to exist as an "ancient tradition."

JA: *So where are we then? Where can we have conversations today about Life, self-discovery, and the creative process?*

GW: Yes, where? . . . I think it's a very important question for many people today. Where can we sit down together for a real inquiry about Life in our society? Where can we "think about our thinking"? Where can we talk about creativity in a way that's not superficial?

So now, to go back to your question, while I'm not fond of labels, I'm comfortable working in the space called the creative field. Having the freedom to look at Life from multiple perspectives is extremely important to me. And I think that's what creativity allows you to do.

But there's more to the picture . . .

Creativity is not static. It's a process that works on multiple levels. Creatives build worlds that redefine how we see reality. In doing so, they alter it. And when they use the vehicle of stories, they help us make sense of our lives. So for me, creativity is transformative and potent, both individually and collectively. And what I love about it is its practical aspect as well. It just can't be theoretical fluff—because at the end of the day, the creative practice must always find applications in the real world. That's why it's so interesting. In that sense, it's the synthesis of imagination and rigor. And I like that a lot.

And so you can say it's a creative philosophy. Creative Dreaming is part of a field I call Depth Creativity. It's a field that lives at the junction between art and spirituality.

LIFE

JA: *In the introduction letter of this book, you say we live in complicated times—we're bombarded with images of violence, greed, and fear.*

GW: Yes, we are. This is obvious.

JA: *Can you expand a little more? Because I know you see it in a unique way.*

GW: Okay. But first, we have to look at it for a meta-perspective and look back in time. Let's pretend we travel in a time machine. And it doesn't matter how far back you want to look. Thirty years ago, one hundred years ago, or a thousand years ago. When you look back at key moments in history, you see a constant. Invariably, history repeats itself—a little bit like an expanding spiral—which is completely weird. The challenges that we are facing today are very real, but they are almost the same as what was happening thirty years ago or a hundred years ago, and so on. It's really strange.

JA: *The same patterns will keep occurring?*

GW: Yes, and it's because you can't alter reality—or create change—if an inner transformation has not occurred first. And as long as we refuse to change inside, there will be no outside transformation.

JA: *But why?*

GW: It's because our inner life has a direct impact on reality. Our personal perspective—just looking at something—literally collapses reality into being; it creates it. This works on a micro or macro level. This also works on both a subjective and objective level. Unless you're able to create authentic change inside, you'll get the same patterns repeating themselves over and over again. That's why Creative Dreaming—in order to work—starts with inner transformation.

JA: *Can you talk about self-acceptance and joy in the*

Creative Dreaming Method?

GW: Yes, this is very important, and they're directly connected. I don't think you can create positive change with hatred. If you say, *"I hate this,"* or *"I hate myself,"* I don't think it's going to work. And so, in the Creative Dreaming Method we always emphasize the idea of joy and self-acceptance because . . . creativity is hard. Maybe we're going to succeed, maybe it's going to take some time . . . with lots of trial and error.

No matter what, always start from this place of self-acceptance and say, *"Hey, I'm trying this today. This is great. And every day I've been working on my project. Good for me."* And then, from this perspective, cultivate your joy, day after day . . . after day . . . after day. You see, most creatives are way too hard on themselves. Very critical to the point where it hurts them. So this loving kindness toward yourself is really important. It's really healthy, too.

THE PERSONA

JA: *In the book, you present a model of the self that includes what you call the Persona. It's an automatic fake-self that you compare to a computer virus. I found the idea scary.*

GW: Yes, it's quite scary. But remember, when you're dealing with scary monsters, humor is key. That's why humor is part of the Creative Dreaming Method. The moment you take your Persona with a grain of salt and you see it for what it really is, it suddenly loses its power.

JA: *How did you come up with this Persona concept?*

GW: First, as I was growing up, I saw it everywhere around me. I saw how some people were driven by ideas that did not make any sense. Ideas that were destroying them. Yet they were deeply attached to the "identity" that was producing these ideas—they would never question it. *"This is who I am"* is a puzzling statement in this context. Even as a child, I realized something was obviously "off." The lack of self-reflective awareness, the automatic thinking, the predictable patterns, the conditioned habits, the status quo mentality . . . while I didn't quite understand what was really going on, I saw there was obviously a problem.

For me, the weirdest part was when I started recognizing patterns. And with these patterns I could predict certain behaviors and results—which is a shocking idea, because from this perspective human life starts more and more to resemble something that's very robotic.

JA: *Did you see it in yourself as well?*

GW: Well, yeah! . . . Automatic patterns for all—including myself! [*Laughs*] This is what led me on a wild chase for understanding and self-knowledge.

JA: *So where did you look to find an answer?*

GW: You know, I really did look everywhere. [*Laughs*] Books, traveling around the world, explorations, encounters, experiences in creative living. My whole life is about this search.

JA: *So, how did you formulate the idea of the Persona?*

GW: This idea is ancient. I saw it under multiple guises in my research; and it's important to acknowledge here what has

influenced the Creative Dreaming Method. First, the Persona
a very common notion in Eastern thought. We've mentioned
Zen before, and it plays a very important role in this tradition.
It also appears in Western traditions. Plato knew about it. It
appears very clearly in Hermetic texts, which have their source
in Ancient Egypt. And much later, when William Shakespeare
wrote, *"All the world's a stage, and all the men and women
merely players,"* he's obviously hinting at a similar concept.
In the twentieth century, you have Gurdjieff, Ouspensky, and
De Ropp. Next, you'll find that Alan Watts, Krishnamurti, and
David Bohm explored this idea as well.

Here, with the Creative Dreaming Method, I'm
reintroducing a complex idea, with deep roots in history, by
synthesizing it for a modern context. But there's more . . .
What's unique in the Creative Dreaming Method is the focus
on the creative process as a tool for transformation. This idea
and the structure of the Method are completely new.

JA: *There's also this connection with the Indian concept of
Maya, right?*

GW: Yes. Our perceived reality (Plato's Cave) is Maya, the illusion. It's a concept that's hard to grasp because, obviously, for
all of us, reality seems totally real. And, in many ways, it is. So
there's a little bit of a paradox there. That's why Plato's Cave is
the perfect prison: We don't see it.

JA: *Yes . . . but what if I do notice that this perceived reality
makes my life miserable?*

GW: Yes! That's it! The act of "noticing." It doesn't seem much
at first, but this is where it all begins. It starts with awareness.
Awareness is always the first step toward freedom. You notice

something. You ask a question. You wake up. That's how you begin your journey.

I think that our collective challenge—as humanity—is our willingness to take a serious look at what we're doing . . . How are we doing, *really*? And based on what we see, we can decide to try new alternatives. It is up to all of us to participate. If we all start taking a new direction, we're going to get different results.

JA: *In the book, you wrote that "the Creative Dreaming Method has revealed a living world where everything is interconnected . . . Can you explain a bit more?*

GW: Yes, this is one of the most important benefits of the Method. Once you realize that the "you" (you think you are) is a relationship. Once you really get that you are connected with everything and everyone, then your relationship with others evolves. It's amazing. You start interacting with other people at a truly authentic level, meaning there's no calculation, no hiding, or secret agenda—you are here *with* them and *for* them, fully present. And what's amazing is that when you're living from this point of view, they feel it, too. And so there's this feedback mechanism that you create with others, that you create with life. It's really transformative. Everything changes.

HOPE FOR CHANGE

JA: *What are your hopes in writing this book?*

GW: My hope with this project is, first, that I'm able to articulate correctly this idea that your life is a playground for growth. That you can dream. That you can contribute. That you can create change . . . That your life today —no matter how mundane it is right now—is an incredible adventure and it's waiting on you to take the first steps. And for this adventure to unfold, you need to change and you need to grow.

Getting a sense of possibilities—that's the first idea.

And after that, my goal is to instill the confidence in the reader to go ahead and try using the Creative Dreaming Method with small creative experiments in every aspect of life.

You can start with something small—see how it works for you—then build forward. The results you'll get bring confidence. This creates what I call "dream with certainty." Because the more you do it, the more you see change happening and it builds this confidence inside of you, this certainty.

JA: *So, to end this conversation, what would you say to a someone who's reading this, at this very moment?*

GW: Hmm . . . [*Long pause*] . . . I would say this . . .

I don't know who you are, or where you are right now, but remember:

Life is change.
Life is waiting for you to embrace change.
Life is asking you to embody change.
Life is inviting you to dream something beautiful.
Life is challenging you to make your dream a reality.
Life is telling you to take a stand for your own life
by creating something new.
Because in doing so, you'll be taking a stand for Life itself.

And now, if you agree with this,

Go for it.
You go for it.

Go for it, and never stop.
Because if you succeed,
then we *all* succeed.

ONCE

UPON A

TIME

Once upon a time, *you* had a little dream,

And it was so tiny . . .
Nothing fantastical, *see?*
But it meant something for you.
So you decided to go for it, thinking:
"Well, let's see what I can do."

They told you, *"But this can't be done, loser!"*
So you did it anyway.
They told you, *"You're just a dreamer!"*
So you kept on dreaming, just to play.

And you moved on,
Many obstacles—gone!
But one day, you fell hard.
And it hurt. It hurt real bad.

They mocked you:
"We told you, Cuckoo!"
But you ignored them all,
You surely know how to take a fall.

And now it's years later. All of this looks so silly.
What was the big fuss, really?
You've dreamed a million dreams—because that's *your* deal.
You've dreamed a million dreams—and *you* made them real.

You thank *everyone* and *everything* that blocked the way,
They all succeeded—didn't they?
By pushing you down, calling you names, and stifling you,
They've made a *bigger dreamer* out of you.

So tomorrow, if you see little ones looking for what's true.
Share what you've learned—will you?
Lower your voice, tell them the secret way.
Reveal, at last, the magical key—if you may:

— *"Reality never stays as it seems,
When* your *soul is empowered by* your *dreams."*

**Tabula rasa
(Blank slate)**

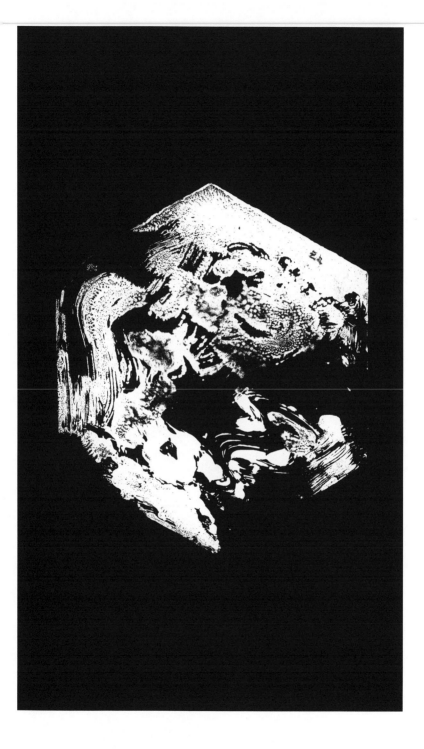

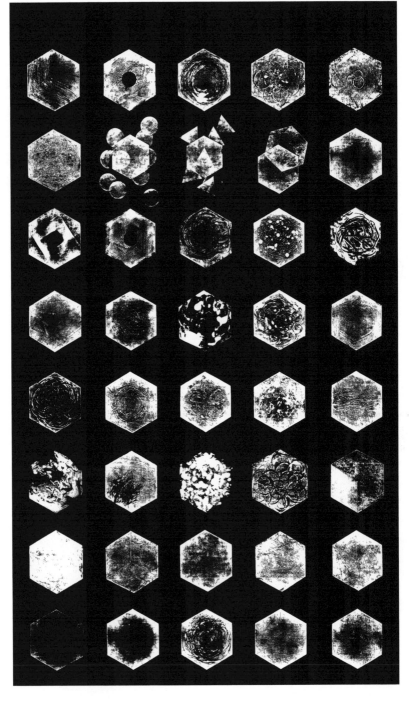

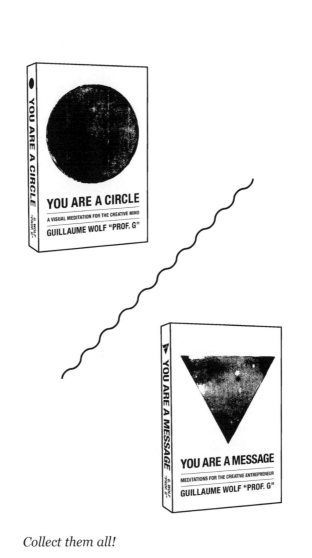

Collect them all!

"GET INVOLVED!"

Hello, my creative friend,

I hope you've enjoyed exploring this book and that it will inspire you to go out there and do great things.

This book and its companions are part of the little experiments I've talked about in this volume.

What you have in your hands *is* an experiment in publishing: <u>It's inspiration, learning, and art combined.</u> **<u>It's a labor of love.</u>**

So if you really like this book and want to see more in the future, get involved! Please join me in this adventure by supporting it.

<u>What you can do:</u>

• Simply post about this book on your social media platform: Use **#YouAreADreamBook**—and you can also tag me on Instagram **@profG.co**.

• Leave a review on **Amazon.com**—and, in your own words, please share your story about how this book is a part of your life— it really helps, and it's super-nice to hear from you.

I really appreciate your support.

Thank you!
Guillaume "Prof. G"

ABOUT THE AUTHOR

Author, teacher, and creativity explorer Guillaume Wolf
"Prof. G" helps creatives dream big dreams, and make them real.

Through his books and online courses, Prof. G's mission is to empower, inspire, and challenge creatives of all walks of life to use their creative skills to bring change in their lives and make a positive impact in the world.

A preeminent expert in applied psychographics, Prof. G is an associate professor at ArtCenter College of Design in Pasadena, California, where he teaches communication design and the psychology of change.

Prof. G is the creator of the Creative Dreaming Method and the founder of the Depth Creativity Institute.

www.ProfG.co

FREE ONLINE CLASS

Are you inspired to go after your dreams and create the life you want?

<u>Here's what to do next:</u>

Take advantage of the free, **Creative Dreaming Intro Course** with Prof. G by reserving your spot now.*

In the **CDM Intro Course**, you'll learn unique Creative Dreaming Method strategies to:

- Boost your creative career today
- Get inspired and gain confidence to create change
- Make this coming year your best year yet

Sign up for your free online video class here:

Visit: **www.profg.co/free**

* Note: Course availability: December 2017. This limited offer is reserved for the readers of *You Are a Dream*. The terms of this offer can be changed at any time.

Made in the USA
Monee, IL
15 May 2020